MORE THAN PETTICOATS

Remarkable Alaska Women

Cherry Lyon Jones

TWODOT®

GUILFORD, CONNECTICUT
HELENA, MONTANA
AN IMPRINT OF THE GLOBE PEQUOT PRESS

To the memory of the pioneer women who made a welcoming, caring place out of "Uncle Sam's Icebox," to the native women who kept their own cultures alive, and especially to the young women who live in Alaska now, so that they do not forget the ones who led the way.

A · TWODOT® · BOOK

Copyright © 2006 by Morris Book Publishing, LLC

TwoDot is a registered trademark of Morris Book Publishing, LLC.

Text design by Nancy Freeborn
Map by M. A. Dubé © Morris Book Publishing, LLC

Library of Congress Cataloging-in-Publication Data
Jones, Cherry Lyon.
  More than petticoats. Remarkable Alaska women / Cherry Lyon Jones.—
1st ed.
        p. cm. — (More than petticoats series)
  Includes bibliographical references.
  ISBN 978-0-7627-3798-7
  1. Women—Alaska—Biography. 2. Women—Alaska—History. 3.
Alaska—Biography. I. Title: Remarkable Alaska women. II. Title. III.
Series.
  CT3262.A4J66 2006
  920.7209798—dc22

                                                                            2005033411

Manufactured in the United States of America
First Edition/Second Printing

CONTENTS

Map iv

Acknowledgments v

Introduction vii

Harriet Smith Pullen, 1860-1947 1

Matilda Kinnon "Tillie" Paul Tamaree, 1860-1952 11

Fannie Sedlacek McKenzie Quigley, 1870-1944 22

Margaret Keenan Harrais, 1872-1964 33

Nellie Neal Lawing, 1873-1956 44

Lois Hudson Allen, 1873-1948 54

Josephine Sather, 1882-1964 65

Crystal Brilliant Snow Jenne, 1884-1968 74

Jessie Spiro Bloom, 1887-1980 85

Clara Hickman Rust, 1890-1978 95

Benzie Ola "Rusty" Dow, 1894-1989 105

Anfesia Shapsnikoff, 1900-1973 115

Bibliography 126

About the Author 134

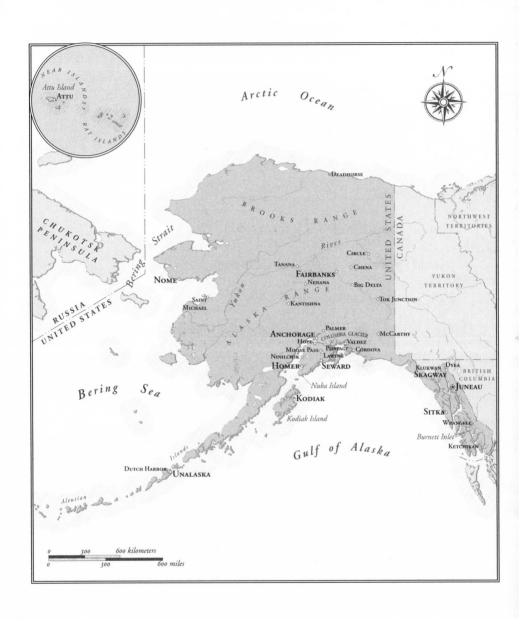

ACKNOWLEDGMENTS

In gathering, sorting, and assimilating information for the writing of this book, the assistance of the following librarians and researchers was invaluable: Arlene Schmuland and Dennis Wall of the Consortium Library at the University of Alaska, Anchorage; Bruce Merrell of the Z. J. Loussac Public Library in Anchorage; Jude Baldwin and Kathleen Hertel of the Anchorage Museum of History and Art; Caroline Atuk and Rose Speranza of the Rasmuson Library at the University of Alaska, Fairbanks; Gladi Kulp of the Alaska State Library in Juneau; and David Wharton of the Museum of Alaska Transportation and Industry in Wasilla; as well as Renee Blahuta from Fairbanks and Tammy Kilgore from Denver.

Special thanks goes to Katherine George of the Homer Public Library in Homer, Alaska, and to Mona Reno of the Nevada State Library in Carson City, Nevada, for their perseverance in locating items through the Interlibrary Loan Program.

The following willingly shared information regarding their relatives and friends:

Barbara Allen, Marilyn Devine Dow, Frances Paul DeGermain, Marion Paul DeWitt, Nana Paul Estus, Ben Paul, and Maxine Selmer. Barbara, Frances, and Maxine additionally helped critique chapters.

Jan Cleere and Jane Haigh offered suggestions and encouragement.

Doug Capra, Lead Interpretive Ranger at Kenai Fjords National Park in Seward, Alaska, provided a wealth of information about Alaska Nellie and Josephine Sather.

I am indebted to Ray Hudson for his suggestions and additions to the chapter on Anfesia Shapsnikoff.

Finally, I am grateful to my family: to my sister, Betty, for critiques and suggestions; to my husband, Fred, for chauffeuring me thousands of miles—two round trips from Minden, Nevada, to Homer, Alaska, and numerous forays around the forty-ninth state— and for proofreading and critiquing (not to mention fixing breakfast every day!); to my daughter, Becky, for accompanying me to Juneau in January and to Fairbanks during a heat wave; and to my son, Dave, for introducing me to Alaska in the first place.

INTRODUCTION

It is rumored that it was a woman, Tagish native Kate Carmack, who first discovered gold in the Yukon in 1896. Of course, at the time, only her white husband could register the claim.

Thousands of gold seekers descended on Alaska in the next few years, many of them women. They came by steamship through the Inland Passage from Seattle and walked the steep trail up and over Chilkoot Pass from Dyea or the White Pass Trail from Skagway. They came overland from Montana through Canada and up the rivers from Nome to the interior. They came with their husbands and they came alone. They mined the land and filed their own claims. Sometimes they took vast riches out of the ground, but just as often took only enough to keep going for the next year, or at least to the next strike. And some of them "mined the miners," finding it easier to provide the room, board, and services that the men needed.

Women came hauling their own supplies, pulling sleds laden with amazing and seemingly out-of-place goods. Anna de Graf was fifty-five years old when she first climbed over Chilkoot Pass in 1894, and she carried with her a sewing machine and a feather bed!

Emily Craig and her husband left Chicago on August 25, 1897, with a party of twelve men and one woman, and a guide who promised to have them in the Klondike within six weeks at a charge of $500 each. The Craigs finally arrived at their destination more than a year later, having suffered untold hardships during the journey. Emily is credited with making the inland territory's first American flag, fashioned from a flour sack, red calico, blue boat paint, and paper stars.

Mollie Walsh ran a little grubstake restaurant in Skagway. When she heard that a young prostitute was ill, she risked a scandal by taking care of her. When the young girl died, Mollie persuaded the pastor of her church to hold a funeral for her. After he gave a moving speech urging others to quit the "profession," Mollie raised money so girls in similar situations could return to Seattle and get a fresh start.

Esther Birdsall Darling lived in Nome from 1907 until 1917. During that time she was co-owner of a kennel that raised the sled dogs that won the first races organized by the Nome Kennel Club. She wrote several books that immortalized the dogs. Also, her poem about the forget-me-not helped establish it as the state flower of Alaska.

Women traveled all over Alaska—alongside the men—worked at every job and helped develop lasting communities by establishing such institutions as schools, churches, libraries, and social clubs. The men of Alaska recognized their contributions and when the first Territorial Legislature met in Juneau in 1913, its first act was to give women the right to vote.

Alaska's modern history began when Russia "discovered" it, and women have played an important part in its development from the very beginning. In the first ship to establish a Russian presence in the new land was the first non-native woman, Natasha Shelikof. When her husband left on expeditions, she was left in charge of the colony established on Kodiak Island in 1784.

At the urging of Secretary of State William H. Seward, the United States purchased Alaska from Russia in 1867 for $7,200,000. The American flag was raised over the territory capital, Sitka, on October 18. Despite such public sentiments as the one printed in the *New York World* that "Russia has sold us a sucked orange," the purchase has certainly proven over the years to be a bargain! Alaska continues to share its mineral riches and natural bounty with the "lower forty-eight." In 1906 the capital was moved to Juneau, where it remains today. Alaska was officially proclaimed the forty-ninth state on January 3, 1959.

Alaskans are a unique people. They refer to any place that is not Alaska as "Outside." Old-timers who have lived in the state long enough to prove their staying power are called "Sourdoughs." Newcomers are "Cheechakos" until they earn the right to be considered real Alaskans.

And, Alaska is huge! Superimposed over a map of the contiguous United States, Alaska, including the Aleutian Islands and southeast panhandle, would reach from the Pacific Ocean of southern California, north to the Canadian border in Minnesota, and extend to the Atlantic Ocean off the southeast coast of South Carolina.

Relocating to this vast land, about which little was known in the early years, required immense fortitude. The women mentioned in this introduction, as well as the ones whose lives are highlighted in this book, represent only a small number of Alaska's fascinating women pioneers. Countless others whose skirts swept the snow—those whose names we know and those who will remain forever anonymous—were all remarkable Alaska women in their own rights.

HARRIET SMITH PULLEN

1860–1947

Elegant Entrepreneur

HARRIET PULLEN STOOD LOOKING at the waves lapping Skagway Beach. The freighter bringing her seven beloved horses from Washington had been forced to anchor in the middle of the harbor due to a lack of space at the docks. After considering the matter for a moment, Harriet made up her mind to go out to the ship and retrieve the animals herself.

With her usual ingenuity, she procured a small boat and rowed out to the anchored vessel. After locating the hatch where her pets waited, she petted and stroked them, and they greeted her with nuzzles and snorts, as happy to see her as she was to see them.

The captain informed her that the animals would have to be unloaded immediately. To his amazement, and over his objections, she replied that she would take them herself. Each would have to be brought up to the deck by sling and pulley. She asked that her favorite, a chestnut named Babe, be first. Returning to her rowboat Harriet called out to Babe, coaxing him to jump from a plank at the edge of the deck. Babe whinnied in fear, but Harriet continued to call, enticing her adored horse into the rough cold waters of Lynn

Canal. Finally, Babe took the plunge and swam trustingly over to the rowboat, where her mistress secured her and rowed the quarter mile back to the safety of the shore. After tying Babe to a large piece of driftwood, Harriet returned to the freighter and repeated the process six more times. When darkness fell all of her horses, plus their packs and harnesses, were on dry land. It was the spring of 1898, and Harriet Pullen had been in Skagway for a little over half a year.

Harriet Smith was born in Wisconsin in 1860. Her parents, Andrew Jackson Smith and Mary Smith, went west, first to the Dakotas and later ending up in La Push, Washington, when Harriet was about sixteen. In 1881, Harriet married Daniel W. Pullen, who ran the local trading post. Over the next several years, the couple had four children: Mildred in 1882, Daniel in 1886, Royal in 1887, and Chester in 1889. The family lived comfortably, and Harriet was indulged with her horses, which she raised from colts and trained lovingly.

Sometime in the mid-1890s, Daniel lost his trading post and the family's large home in a court fight over the homestead, and the Pullens fell on hard times. Harriet felt compelled to leave her husband and seek a new life for herself and her children. Arriving in Seattle in 1897, she found the cry of "Gold in the Klondike!" resounding throughout the town. Catching a bit of the "gold fever," and sensing an opportunity for a new life ahead, she left her children with family and headed north to Alaska, identifying herself to fellow travelers as a widow.

Harriet arrived in Skagway on September 12, 1897, aboard the steamer *Rosalie*. Because docks had yet to be built, passengers were unloaded into small boats and deposited on the beach, along with piles of their belongings. Although the rush to the Klondike had started a scant two months earlier, Skagway was already a bustling, rowdy town of tents along makeshift streets, with a few hastily erected wooden structures.

MRS. PULLEN, LEANING ON A BRIDGE
ON THE GROUNDS OF PULLEN HOUSE

With $7.00 in her pocket, Harriet dragged her luggage up the beach past the tide line and sat down to contemplate her next move. As she watched the ill-mannered gold seekers and listened to their crude language, she began to wonder if she had made the right decision, coming alone to this wild place. One very loud voice stood out above the others, and she looked up to see a large man moving from one group to the next. It was Captain William Moore, the original Skagway townsite owner.

"Is there a cook anywhere? Can anybody cook?" He noticed Harriet sitting alone. "Can you cook?" he demanded.

"Yes, I can," she answered, although she had never cooked for anyone except her own family.

He took her arm and led her up the beach, into a large tent where there was a sheet metal stove and a long table with benches. The walls were lined with boxes, and she could hardly stand up for the hams and bacon slabs hanging from the ridgepole. Piles of dirty dishes sat on the shelves. Scraps of food littered the floor.

"Cook quit," he announced. "I'll pay three dollars a day. My men are building the wharves down on the beach, and they'll be mighty hungry. You'll have eighteen for dinner." And with that, he strode out the door.

Harriet sat down at the table, put her head in her arms, and sobbed. Then she pulled herself together, stood up to her full 5 feet 9 inches, brushed off her fashionable princess-style dress, tied up her unruly red hair, strung a flour sack around her waist, and went to work. She scrubbed the dishes with ashes, raked the floor, and put together dinner for eighteen men. With sudden inspiration, she cooked some dried apples, rolled out a piecrust, pounded out a pie plate from an old tin can, and made the first of what would become her signature apple pies.

After a few days she began to realize that her wages would not be enough to bring her children to Skagway any time soon. She augmented her income by baking apple pies and selling them for a tidy sum to miners preparing to make their way up White Pass Trail. Harriet cooked and baked, and before Christmas she was able to send for her two older boys to join her in the little log house that she now called home. Their father accompanied them, leaving fifteen-year-old Mildred to finish her schooling in Ellensburg, Washington, since rough Skagway was no place for a young girl. The youngest child, Chester, also remained in Washington.

All that long winter Harriet cooked and baked. She once said that she had made enough dried-apple pies "to cover the trail from the middle of town to the top of Chilkoot Pass." In the spring she took her winter profits and sent for those seven horses she had reluctantly left behind.

Harriet quit cooking and launched her next project, a freighting business. At the time, she was the only woman to attempt that risky venture. She would load up a four-horse wagon, drive it to the bottom of the pass, and transfer the goods to the backs of her horses. Carefully and slowly, she would lead them up the steep rocky trail to the top, collect twenty-five dollars from the owners, and then make the return trip for another load.

The single-file trail to the top of Chilkoot Pass was rocky and treacherous, and the horses had to be fitted with special "corked" shoes with sharp studs to help keep their footing. If one of the creatures stumbled, "corked" (cut) itself, and was unable to continue, it would be shot, and the carcass pushed over the edge into the canyon below. Urged on by desperate, gold-hungry men, many overladen and underfed animals collapsed and died on the trail. The gorge with hundreds of carcasses piled on the rocks below soon became known as Dead Horse Canyon.

Into this melee, Harriet took her precious pets. Leading them carefully and treating them gently, she maneuvered the trail countless times without mishap and was able to earn enough money to support herself and her family. After a toll road was built up the pass, she was able to take her horse-drawn wagon and haul more goods on each trip.

On one of these wagon trips, as she later told the story, her horses became entangled with a runaway wagon coming from the opposite direction. Her favorite horse, Babe, corked herself and was permanently crippled. Harriet paid for Babe to be transported back to the States, where she was cared for until her death.

In 1898, construction began on the White Pass and Yukon Route Railroad. Harriet knew that completion of the line would mean the end of her freighting business, and she began to consider another means of supporting herself and her family. In the meantime, she continued to bake and sell her delicious apple pies.

When gold was discovered nearby in Atlin, British Columbia, Harriet decided to try her luck at prospecting. She and another younger woman took off up the White Pass Trail planning to ride two of her horses to the top then send them back down to Skagway. But when a man offered her ten dollars to carry his supplies, she loaded up the horses, collected the money, and walked up the trail. At the top of the pass was Lake Bennett, where a bustling camp had sprung up as prospectors struggled to build rafts or find other ways to cross the lake. One man had set up a small sawmill and was building boats for one hundred dollars each. Harriet bought one of his boats, giving him the ten dollars that she had just earned as a down payment. She then recruited ten men to crew the boat across the lake, charging them each ten dollars, with which she paid for the boat. When she arrived on the opposite shore, she owned a boat and had money in her pocket!

Unfortunately, Harriet's prospecting plans were ruined when she fell and broke her wrist. She returned across the lake, again charging passengers to crew, and then sold the boat and returned to Skagway with money to spare.

In the spring of 1899, when Mildred finished her schooling in Seattle, Harriet sent for her to join the family. Little Chester was also in Skagway by then. Her husband, Daniel did not like Alaska, and stayed in Skagway only long enough to be counted in the first census in 1900 as the "head" of the Pullen family. He then traveled to southeast Alaska, before returning to Washington, where he died in 1910.

In 1900, Captain Moore had constructed a showcase house for himself but had never occupied it. He subsequently offered Harriet the opportunity to lease it. Realizing the possibilities this opened for her, she immediately accepted, and in 1902 the Pullen House Hotel was born. A "hotel-worth" of furniture, which had been brought to Skagway for a hotel that never opened, was in storage, and Harriet arranged to rent it, with an agreement to purchase it in the future.

Even before her hotel opened, every room was rented; Pullen House was successful from the beginning. Harriet's cooking skills were well known, and she furnished the rooms simply but comfortably. Pleased with her accomplishment, Harriet made plans to purchase the furniture. But the owner suddenly appeared with a wagon one morning and took it all away to open a hotel of his own, since hers had done so well. Undaunted, Harriet ordered lumber and boxes, hired some men and tools, and by evening every room had a box dresser, box chair, and rough bedstead. Fortunately, she already owned the mattresses and bedding. When she explained her predicament, every guest loyally agreed to stay and put up with the makeshift furniture until it could be replaced.

Within a year Pullen House was so profitable that Harriet was able to purchase the building from Captain Moore. She soon also purchased land for a small farm across the bay on the old townsite of Dyea, where she raised a herd of dairy cattle. These cows provided fresh cream, which the guests of the hotel skimmed for themselves from blue-enameled pans in the pantry.

Margaret Murie remembered staying at Pullen House in 1911 on her way to Fairbanks when she was nine years old: "The guest was given a bowl and a spoon and allowed to skim off cream for his porridge and coffee. Skimming your own cream at Pullen House in the land of no cream was a ritual talked of all over the North in those days."

Even as the gold rush days subsided and the population of Skagway dwindled, Pullen House continued to serve travelers who arrived by ship and by the White Pass and Yukon Route Railroad (WP&YR). Harriet, always the gracious dignified hostess, became known as "Ma Pullen" to her ever-growing clientele of construction workers, geologists, salesmen, and government officials, along with their families.

Harriet also began collecting and displaying interesting bits of Alaskana for her guests, realizing that she was saving items from history that might otherwise have been lost. Eventually her curio room held such items as hand-hammered Russian copper, silver candlesticks from Baranof Castle at Old Sitka, and rare purple-blue Russian glass beads made especially for the early fur trade. She displayed the first newspaper heralding the great Dawson gold strike and surrounded it with rocks painted gold to represent huge nuggets. The craps table, roulette wheels, and oak gambling table that belonged to Soapy Smith, Skagway's famous gangster from the stampede days, were there, and Harriet often regaled her guests with tales of Soapy's exploits. She had also collected numerous native artifacts, including a medicine man's mask, tobacco pouches made from white swans' feet, and bags of cedar bark, as well as moose robes and coats. She enjoyed dressing in the native costumes and telling stories of early Skagway days.

Pullen House was renowned throughout the North for its elegance, both inside and out. The building itself sat amidst stretches of green lawn, intersected by streams flowing into small ponds where ducks swam happily. There were flowerbeds filled with hollyhocks and forget-me-nots, and a garden seat was nestled against a lattice laced with sweet peas. Inside the guestrooms came complete with a featherbed and a bathtub; the banquet hall tables were set with Haviland china and a silver service of Harriet's own design. The food served was simple, but fresh, and came primarily from her farm in Dyea.

Many famous signatures could be found in the Pullen House guest register, including those of Jack London and Robert Service. President Warren G. Harding, although he did not stay at Pullen House, spoke from the veranda when he visited Skagway in July of 1923.

Harriet Pullen, along with Martin Itjen, who operated a streetcar tour business, was credited with helping develop the Alaskan tourist trade. They convinced cruise ships to stop in Skagway long enough for their passengers to ride the WP&YR train to the top of the pass and back.

Mr. Itjen loved to tell the story about a Pullen House guest who once asked one of Ma Pullen's little sons (possibly grandsons), "How do you pronounce the streetcar man's name?"

Dignified Harriet was horrified to hear him respond, "It's itchin'. You know, like itchin' and scratchin'!"

Although Harriet undoubtedly would have liked to have her sons stay and help with her business, she sent them Outside to get the best schooling they could. Royal graduated from the University of Washington and became a mechanical engineer. He married and raised his family in Lead, South Dakota. Dan graduated from the same school and went on to be the first cadet from Alaska to attend West Point. Both Dan and Royal served in World War I and earned many medals, which they sent home to their mother. Chester drowned in a swift river while on his way back to university in 1912. Royal lived to be over one hundred years old. He died in California in 1990.

Mildred married and moved Outside. She had a daughter, Mary, and three sons. Mary returned to Skagway and was raised by Harriet, who adopted her. The three boys also spent time at Pullen House, as did Harriet's other grandchildren from South Dakota.

Harriet Pullen continued to promote tourism at every opportunity and tout the virtues of visiting Alaska. The local newspaper, the *Skagway Cheechako,* noted in its February 13, 1937 edition:

> Mrs. Harriet S. Pullen of the Pullen House, who is now in Seattle, broadcasted over NBC in a coast to coast hook-up, on Sunday afternoon January 17. She was a guest on the L.C. Smith Typewriter program. She gave an interesting talk on Skagway and told the world that Skagway was the best place to live in the world from the standpoint of health, climate, and scenery.

According to the *Cheechako,* on that same trip, Harriet "addressed the students at the University of Washington in Seattle." The Alaska-Yukon pioneers in Seattle observed "Skagway Night" while she was there, and the *Cheechako* reported, "It has been announced that none other than Mrs. Harriet S. Pullen will 'frame' an apple pie, from the original Skagway recipe."

Harriet Pullen often drove the horses pulling her distinctive coach that carried guests to her hotel, and well into her later years, she met every ship that docked at Skagway. She died in 1947, four days before her eighty-seventh birthday, and is buried near the site of her famous Pullen House.

As Mary Davis wrote in her 1930 book, *Uncle Sam's Attic:* "No one knows Skagway who does not know Harriet Pullen. For years she has *been* Skagway, to all who stop and linger there to hear from her own vigorous dramatic lips the tale of Skagway's tarnished day of glory."

And Harriet Pullen was quite a storyteller! She often recounted her 1897 arrival in Skagway, a "widow" with seven dollars to her name and four young children to support. She described her joy at sending for her three little redheaded boys and at finally seeing them asleep peacefully on beds of straw. She told of her famous apple pies baked in hammered-out tin cans, of making drinking glasses from discarded beer bottles. Perhaps she exaggerated her tales of derring-do on the White Pass Trail, or her difficulties starting her hotel, but there is no doubt Harriet Pullen was a true Alaska pioneer, with that indomitable spirit ingrained in the women who came North. She brought gentility and social graces to a wild land.

MATILDA KINNON "TILLIE" PAUL TAMAREE

1860–1952

Tlingit Missionary and Leader

UNDER COVER OF DARKNESS a young Tlingit woman crept out of a house in Victoria, British Columbia, and stealthily made her way along the dirt road toward the water. She carried her younger daughter and urged her older one to hurry quietly along with her. At the water's edge, her clansman waited in a small canoe. After handing over her few personal possessions and her precious daughters, the woman climbed into the canoe and started her long journey north.

Traveling only at night, and hiding during the day, the group covered 600 miles along the "Inside Passage" of Alaska, until they arrived safely in the land of the Stikeen-quan near Wrangell.

This escape allowed Matilda Kinnon and her older sister, Margaret, to avoid being sent to Scotland, where their father's family would have cared for them. Their mother, Kut-XooX, was ill with the "coughing sickness" (tuberculosis). Overhearing her husband's plan to send the children overseas, she vowed to find a way to return them to her own relatives, where they would be reared in the proper Tlingit tradition.

So Kut-XooX fled, taking her girls to her sister, Xoon-sel-ut, who was married to Chief Snook, of the Stikeen-quan. But soon after their arrival, Kut-XooX died. A potlatch, or community feast, was held to honor her life, and in a special ceremony, the two little girls were given Tlingit names. Matilda was given the name Kah-thli-yudt. She came to be called Kah-tah-ah and was adopted by Chief Snook. Margaret was named Tsoon-klah. She went to live with her mother's brother in the nearby Tee-hit-ton village. After the naming ceremony, the "taint of white blood" was considered "wiped out forever," although as an adult, Kah-tah-ah (later named Tillie) always said that it didn't work.

Soon after her mother's death an important and prophetic event occurred in little Kah-tah-ah's life. She, too, became ill with the "coughing sickness." Snook, fearing she might die, took her to the shaman, Shquindy. Shquindy had long, black hair with one contrasting white lock over his forehead. It was neither combed nor cut, and he was very frightening. Snook laid Kah-tah-ah gently on the mat in front of the shaman and stepped back. After performing his healing rituals, Shquindy announced that Kah-tah-ah would recover, have children, and live to an old age; she would "do special work among her people and would be much loved by them." Then Snook took her home, where she recovered and grew strong.

Kah-tah-ah had a happy childhood as the beloved and privileged daughter of Chief Snook, who brought her up in the old Tlingit ways. When she was about twelve years old, a marriage was arranged for her with a Christian Tsimshian chief who named himself Abraham Lincoln. Snook did not want Kah-tah-ah to be married so young and sent so far away, and Kah-tah-ah certainly did not want to marry this man who was twenty-seven years older than she! But Lincoln sent many gifts to Snook requesting Kah-tah-ah as his bride. Also, Lincoln was Eagle clan and Kah-tah-ah was Raven clan, so the match would be acceptable. Traditionally, Tlingits are divided

MATILDA KINNON "TILLIE" PAUL TAMAREE

into two clans, Wolf/Eagle (or Eagle) and Raven. All members of a clan are considered to be brothers and sisters, so to marry inside the clan would be considered incest.

Snook decided to allow Lincoln to take Kah-tah-ah to Tongass, with the understanding that he would not force her into matrimony unless she agreed. The journey took three long weeks by canoe and when she reached her destination, she was even more determined not to marry the chief. A girl in the village told her, "We are Christians here, and we follow the white man's laws. So if you do not want to marry a man, no one can force you to do so."

The word circulated that Kah-tah-ah did not want to marry, and Lincoln called a council. He stated that if Kah-tah-ah announced before them that she did not want to marry him, he would release her from the marriage arrangement. Kah-tah-ah said "no" in front of the council and Lincoln was true to his word.

Kah-tah-ah then went to live with the Methodist missionary, Reverend Thomas Crosby, and his wife in Port Simpson. There she learned for the first time about the white man's God and Jesus. The Crosbys called her Sarah, not knowing she already had an English name, Matilda.

Kah-tah-ah was quick to relearn English, as it had been the language of her infancy. Even though she was busy, communicative, and appeared happy, she was very homesick. She even tried to escape, stealing away in a canoe one dark night, just as her mother had done many years ago. But the Crosbys sent rescuers to find her and bring her back safely.

In 1877 the first woman missionary to Alaska, Amanda McFarland, arrived in Wrangell. Although Snook still disapproved of the "white man's ways," he contacted Reverend Crosby and promised that if he sent Kah-tah-ah back to Wrangell, she would attend school with the "lady missionary."

Realizing how homesick their "Sarah" was, the Crosbys returned her to Wrangell, and she went to live in Mrs. McFarland's Presbyterian Home and School for Girls. She reclaimed her English name of Matilda Kinnon and was called Tillie.

At the school Tillie soon learned to read and write. Mrs. McFarland wrote to Sheldon Jackson, the Presbyterian missionary who later became Alaska's first General Superintendent of Education, "Our oldest girl in the Home (Tillie Kinnon) has become a Christian, and expresses a great desire to be trained for a teacher. She is already quite a help in teaching the younger children. She is a girl of much promise and decision of character."

Reverend S. Hall Young arrived in Wrangell in 1878 and organized a Presbyterian church there. Tillie became his interpreter. On Saturday afternoons she would meet with him to hear the lesson for the following day's sermon, so she would be prepared to translate it. One afternoon Reverend Young read the story of the great flood to Tillie. She sat very quietly, with no comment. Finally, he asked, "Do you not understand the story, Tillie?"

She answered, "Yes, of course, I do. But if I tell this story to my people, they won't believe me. It rains here for forty days and forty nights all the time, and our land has never been flooded!"

In fact, Tillie found there were several biblical passages that would have been unbelievable to the Tlingit people. According to family lore, it wasn't unusual for the congregation to hear from Tillie a different Bible text from the one being taught by Reverend Young, who couldn't understand what Tillie was saying in her translation.

One day a handsome young Tlingit/French-Canadian named Louis Paul (Peyreau) stopped at Wrangell on his way home from the Cassiar gold fields. Tillie and Louis were attracted to one another immediately, and he ended up staying in Wrangell. Soon he joined Tillie's church, and in January of 1882, the couple married in a Christian ceremony performed by Reverend Young.

Snook was extremely disappointed that Louis did not come to him in the traditional Tlingit manner, bringing gifts in a symbolic show of respect for the bride's family. He further disapproved of the fact that Tillie did not have a proper Tlingit wedding. But, at least, Louis belonged to the Wolf/Eagle clan. Now Tillie Paul's missionary work began in earnest.

Six months after their wedding, the Presbyterian Board of Home Missions sent the Pauls, the first native couple so commissioned, to minister to the Tlingits living at the north end of the Inside Passage. The village of Klukwan was very remote and was accessible only by canoe. By the time winter came Louis had built a snug little log house, as well as a school. While Tillie taught at the school, Louis built the church. Bringing the gospel to Klukwan was a challenge. The people there still believed in shamanism and practiced witchcraft to cure illnesses. Still, as Tillie and Louis were both high-ranking in their respective tribes, they were received with hospitality in the village. Although these Tlingits were among the last to embrace the white man's culture, the Pauls wrote in an article for a national Presbyterian bulletin, "All the Indians say they were sorry a teacher did not come amongst them sooner; that by this time they would know more about God."

By the following summer their first child was due, and Tillie wanted to be near her family. They returned to Wrangell, where their first son, Samuel Kendall, made his appearance in August.

After Samuel's birth, the mission board sent the Pauls to Tongass at the south end of the Inside Passage, near Louis's family home. His grandfather, Yashnoosh, was greatly pleased to see him again and to greet his wife and new baby.

When the Pauls' second son was born with one shock of hair lighter than the rest, Tillie gave him the Tlingit name of Shquindy, after the old shaman, and the English name, William Lewis.

Tillie continued to teach school, to preach to the congregation, and to do all the work of a teacher and pastor. Louis supplemented Tillie's part-time missionary salary with hunting and trapping. Tillie and Louis were proud of the work they were doing and were happy and content.

Around this time, plans were being made to establish a "model" Christian town in which two tribes, the Cape Fox and the Tongass, would live together. An area south of present-day Ketchikan was being considered. In December of 1886, Louis Paul, Samuel Saxman, who was a government schoolteacher, and a native named Edgar, left in a canoe to survey the site and report on its suitability. They were never heard from again.

Tillie was devastated. She was left with two little boys, one of them just a toddler, and another baby was on the way. Without Louis it would be impossible for her to continue the missionary work in Tongass. Snook had died and she had no other close relatives.

Among her people there was an undercurrent of belief that the drowning had not been accidental. The weather had been clear and Louis was both an excellent seaman and swimmer. It was almost more than Tillie could bear. With all this weighing on her young shoulders, Tillie's baby son was born prematurely, but healthy. She named him Louis Francis Paul in honor of his father.

Tillie was at a loss as to how she was going to support herself and her boys. Dr. Sheldon Jackson was aware of Tillie's plight and invited her to join the staff of the Sitka Industrial and Training School, which he had started in 1878 for Tlingit students.

At first this would seem like the perfect answer for Tillie. But the tribes of Sitka and Wrangell had a long-standing feud; distrust of the Sitka people had been ingrained in Tillie since she was a small child. Nevertheless, Tillie took her boys and set out bravely for Sitka, determined to be a peacemaker in the Christian manner. This attitude served her well, and in future church disagreements, Tillie's mediating skills were often utilized.

Tillie Paul remained as a staff member at the school in Sitka for about seventeen years. During that time her accomplishments were legion.

An excellent seamstress since childhood, she was placed in charge of the sewing room. She organized and ran the laundry, even helping the older girls wash everything by hand one winter when the boiler failed to work and the water had to be heated over fires. When the boys' hospital was opened in 1890, she was the nurse. Her work there was so valuable that when the new infirmary was opened in 1926, it was named "Tillie Paul Manor" in her honor. At one point, when there was no one available who could play the church organ, Tillie taught herself to play and was soon accompanying even the most difficult hymns. She translated many of the standard hymns and scriptures into Tlingit. Additionally, she joined forces with her cousin, Frances Willard, and the two of them wrote the Tlingit language into English sounds and created a dictionary.

But even with her emphasis on Tlingit, Tillie knew English would be the language of the future. In Alaska, as in the rest of the United States, it was believed by educators that the white man's culture could only be taught using the white man's English, and native children were actually punished for speaking their own languages.

Bearing all this in mind, Tillie made the difficult decision to send her young boys to the Carlisle Indian School in Pennsylvania. This would mean a long separation, as it was so far away and travel was so difficult that the children would not be able to return for vacations, nor even for the summers.

Having seen the terrible effect of alcohol abuse on her people, Tillie joined with another staff member at the school to start a temperance organization. She was adamant about attending the group's weekly meetings, and walked the mile into town no matter the weather.

These prayer meeting services grew into the New Covenant Legion. The importance of this organization cannot be overemphasized. Begun as a temperance and prayer group, the organization also advocated other Christian works. Members distributed food baskets to the needy, fed and ministered to the sick, and worked to change some of the old customs that ran against the grain of church teachings. But most significantly, in 1912, the Legion's founders expanded the organization to become the Alaska Native Brotherhood (ANB). The ANB to this day has had an enormous effect on Alaska native people, working constantly for equality in land ownership, schooling, voting, and other basic rights. In 1920 Tillie organized an affiliated group, the Alaska Native Sisterhood, or ANS.

Tillie was a strong force in the Presbyterian Church and traveled extensively on its behalf. She twice traveled to New York City to attend the General Assembly and speak up for, among other things, the role of women in the church. In 1902 she was invited to address the General Assembly and—according to an article published in 1988, a copy of which is in the national Presbyterian archives—she was possibly the first woman to do so. She was also appointed a church lay worker and did work in both Kake and Petersburg, on Kupreanof Island, north of Wrangell.

In 1903 the Presbyterian Board of Home Missions sent Tillie to the Wrangell Presbyterian Church to "help heal a breach in the church there." Two years later she married an elder in the church, William Baptiste Tamaree, a Tlingit/French-Canadian, as Louis Paul had been.

It annoyed Tillie that even though she did much missionary work, her reports to the Presbytery had to be signed by a man in order for them to be "legal." Therefore, it was with joy that she was ordained an elder of the Wrangell church in 1931. She was the first woman to be so honored in the Alaska-Northwest Synod, and one of the first in the country after the General Assembly approved women as elders in 1930. She was one of the few workers to be given a fifty-year pin for missionary service.

Tillie could also be considered a civil rights activist. The Alaska legislature had given the right to vote to those who were U.S. citizens, which did not, at the time, include natives. In 1923 she encouraged her friend, Charlie Jones, to go to the polls. They were both indicted by a grand jury, Jones for "voting illegally" and Tillie for "aiding and abetting illegal voting." Her son, William Paul, successfully defended Jones and the charges against Tillie were dropped. In 1924 all Native Americans were granted U. S. citizenship.

Tillie lived in Wrangell for the rest of her life. She and William had three daughters—but only one, Frances, survived. Tillie's oldest son, Samuel, remained in the eastern United States and she visited him whenever she could. When she was there, she had her feet measured and Samuel sent her new shoes every Christmas. William Lewis Paul returned to Alaska and became the first native lawyer in the territory. He married a white woman, Frances Lackey, who wrote a children's book based on Tillie's Tlingit childhood.

Louis Francis Paul became a newspaper editor in Petersburg, Alaska. He married Mathilda Jones. This caused quite a stir in both of their families, as they were both Raven clan. Two of Tillie's granddaughters, Nana Paul Estus and Marian Paul deWitt, tell this story from their parents' reminiscences:

> It was a rainy October night when Louis brought his new bride home to Tillie and William Tamaree. Tillie refused to let them in the house because they had broken an Indian law, which had had very serious consequences. In the old ways they would have been shunned and ostracized, even killed.
>
> Grandpa Tamaree, in one of the few times that he spoke forcefully to Tillie, chastised her, "You teach about Christian life and want our children to get an education and practice the white man's ways. That is just what Louis and Mathilda are doing!"

Matilda Kinnon Paul Tamaree died at her home in Wrangell on August 20, 1952. According to obituaries in the *Wrangell Sentinel* and the Sheldon Jackson College newsletter, *The Verstovian,* she was ninety years old. According to her granddaughter, Frances Paul DeGermain, the family places her birth date as 1860, which would have made her ninety-two when she died.

Throughout her life Tillie Paul Tamaree maintained love and respect for both her old Tlingit culture and her new Christian life. She spoke out for the rights of women and Alaska natives. She was farsighted in her understanding that the "old ways" must adapt and incorporate the "new ways" if her people were to reach their full potential in society. She created a bridge between the old and new ways, that they might work together rather than have one supersede the other. As the shaman, Shquindy, had predicted those many years ago, she "did special work among her people and was much loved by them."

Reverend S. Hall Young wrote of her, "Tillie Paul Tamaree remains the most influential native woman in Alaska, the spiritual mother of her people, the example bright and shining of what Christianity can accomplish in a most difficult mission field."

FANNIE SEDLACEK
MCKENZIE QUIGLEY

1870-1944

Storytelling Hostess of Kantishna

A SMALL, WIRY WOMAN CREPT STEALTHILY toward Moose Creek where the creek meandered across the wide expanse of tundra beneath mighty Mt. McKinley. Catching sight of a large bull caribou, the woman raised her gun and fired. The animal disappeared behind a clump of willows. Assuming she had missed, she lowered her firearm just as another bull appeared. Raising the gun quickly, she fired off another shot. The second caribou stumbled toward the creek, where it was joined by the first. The two animals made their way unsteadily to the middle of the ice-laden water, where they both collapsed, dead.

The woman waded into the slush ice and tied one end of a rope to the caribou; the other end she fastened to a clump of willows. With the carcasses thus secure, she proceeded to butcher the animals and cache the meat in her food tunnels up the ridge, near her house. Fannie Quigley's husband, Joe, was in the hospital in Fairbanks, recovering from a mine cave-in, and sixty-year-old Fannie had just provided their meat supply for the winter.

Fannie Sedlacek was born into the Bohemian community of Wahoo, Nebraska, on March 18, 1870. As a young woman she left home and traveled west. She earned her way by cooking and house-keeping and learning English as she went. In 1898 she joined the gold rush stampede over Chilkoot Pass, along with thousands of other fortune-seekers.

As the creeks around Dawson began to be claimed and staked, Fannie intuitively arrived at each new location to set out her MEALS FOR SALE sign. She dished up plates of beans and bacon and poured mugs of coffee, all cooked over her portable Yukon stove. Her knack for arriving first on the scene led to her nickname, "Fannie the Hike." She did her fair share of prospecting as well, but feeding the miners proved to be a more reliable form of income.

One of the miners she fed was the Canadian, Angus McKenzie. After they returned from two "rushes" in 1900, Fannie and Angus were married in Dawson on October 1. By the next year Angus was helping Fannie run a roadhouse on Hunker Creek. But the marriage seemed doomed from the start. Angus was a drinker and was known to knock Fannie around. Fannie was a heavy drinker, as well, and remained so her entire life.

So in January of 1903 when word reached Dawson of the Tanana gold strike, Fannie started out on a 700-mile trek alongside the Yukon River to Rampart. By spring she was ready to either feed the miners, do some prospecting herself, or both.

It was about this time that Fannie first met Joe Quigley. Joe was from Pennsylvania and had come to Alaska in 1891. He had prospected in all the hot spots and was aiming for Tanana, when he became ill with typhoid fever. Fannie reportedly nursed him back to health.

In 1905 Joe and his partner, Jack Horn, discovered gold in Kantishna, on the north side of Mt. McKinley. The next year, Fannie also arrived in Kantishna where, on the banks of Glacier Creek, she opened "Mrs. McKenzie's Roadhouse" and fed the miners all winter. Soon she and Joe Quigley had become partners, both professionally and romantically. Both filed and worked claims on Glacier Creek, Caribou Creek, and other nearby locations. Although Fanny often insisted that Joe's job was to work the mines and hers was to take care of the house and the camp, she did her share of mine work too. For several years she continued to stake claims using her legal name of McKenzie. Angus McKenzie did not appear again in Fannie's life, and his fate is unknown.

The stampede that had brought hordes of gold-seekers to Kantishna in 1905 was over within two or three years. Most of the miners had moved on, but Fannie and Joe remained on Glacier Creek year-round, eking out small amounts from their placer claims. Joe also continued to prospect in the hills, ever hopeful for a big pay-off.

The year that Fannie arrived in Kantishna was also the year that she shot her first moose and started on the path to a skilled wilderness lifestyle. She became an excellent hunter and delighted in telling one story in particular that highlighted her exploits over those of Joe's.

According to Fannie, she and Joe had gone hunting and Joe had returned with no game, while she had bagged two caribou, a bear, and a moose. Arriving home, she tossed him her skirt and told him, "Here, you do the housework. I'm the hunter in the family. Gimme your pants!"

However, not all hunts met with success. When Charles Sheldon, the well-known big-game hunter and naturalist, came to Denali in the summer of 1907 to spend the year studying the Dall mountain sheep, he stayed with the Quigleys on his way into the field. The following February, Fannie and Joe spent sixteen days at his camp, hunting almost every day. Sheldon noted in his journal: "On this day I went hunting with Mrs. Quigley and after an arduous mountain climb, which she made as easily as any man, we came close to a band of thirty-four sheep; but her rifle missed fire twice,

FANNIE QUIGLEY HOLDING A GIANT RHUBARB

and then she missed them running." In the end, however, Joe and Fannie were successful, and the trip ultimately yielded "two ewes and a yearling ram."

After Fannie and Joe set up housekeeping together, Fannie didn't go into town in Fairbanks for seven years. At first, there were other women in the mining community. They came with their husbands, or as prospectors themselves, to run boarding houses or to feed the miners. But after 1909, Fannie was the only woman living in the Kantishna district. She and Joe prospected, and Fannie perfected her hunting, trapping, gardening, cooking, and wilderness skills.

Each household had to be responsible for providing its own sustenance throughout the year, so many of the miners tended gardens. But Fannie's garden became something of a masterpiece. Although

Alaska has a very short growing season of about ten weeks at the altitude where Fannie gardened, it is enhanced by the extended daylight of the summer, and Fannie not only took advantage of that, but also used other methods that ensured success. She planted in areas of the best sunlight exposure and lined the garden plots with rocks to absorb more of the sun's heat and keep the soil warm during the brief summer nights.

Many visitors to the area, whether on mining business or seeking adventure in the mountains, stopped to visit the Quigleys. Fannie often fed members of expeditions attempting to conquer Mt. McKinley. In fact, over the years it became somewhat of a tradition for McKinley's climbing parties to visit Fannie and Joe. Belmore Browne stopped on his way back from a 1912 summit attempt and wrote quite a bit about Fannie's cabin, her cooking, garden, and food storage tunnels. He described her as "one of the most remarkable women I have ever met" and praised the magnificent meal she had prepared, waxing eloquent about the accompaniment to the corned moose roast, the "moose muffle jelly," made from the animal's nose and lips!

Outside the cabin window Fannie grew flowers. Her immense pansies glowed with brilliant colors that she preserved by pressing them between the pages of heavy books. During the long winter hours, she worked to recreate the flowers in embroidery, using the skill learned as a child from her Bohemian relatives in Nebraska. Poppies and wildflowers also grew in profusion around the house.

Below the cabin was the vegetable garden. A U.S. Geological Survey geologist, Stephen Capps, visited the Quigleys in 1916, and wrote in his field notebook about Fannie's garden. He listed mature cauliflower, cabbage, great heads of lettuce, radishes, onions, 2½-inch new potatoes, rhubarb, rutabagas, cucumbers, and even ripe tomatoes, all ready by the first of August! In February of 1916, Fannie was inducted into the Pioneer Women of Alaska in Fairbanks, whose members had to have come to the territory before 1908. For Fannie this was welcome recognition of her years spent carving a comfortable home out of the barren wilderness.

After almost twelve years of partnership, Fannie and Joe were finally officially married at Glacier Creek on February 2, 1918. The commissioner for the Kantishna recording district, J. C. Van Orsdel, performed the ceremony, and rumor has it that he used a Montgomery Ward catalog in lieu of a Bible. Shortly thereafter Fannie and Joe moved to a new location that came to be known as Quigley Ridge. They built their house and a number of outbuildings on a steep hillside overlooking the junction of Moose Creek and Friday Creek.

Once again Fannie set about developing a garden. The rich soil that had helped make her first garden so successful was near the creeks, so Fannie hauled it in by dog team in the winter. When she needed it, she brought more soil in by backpack during the summer. Her soil-warming rock system also served to terrace the steep ground to make wider planting beds.

In 1925 Grant Pearson, a young ranger at nearby Mt. McKinley National Park, met Fannie and was astonished to see her food storage tunnels. Joe had dug a tunnel into the permafrost, and when it didn't pan out as a mine, Fannie converted it into a frozen food locker. With a series of doors, the temperature stayed cold enough that food could be frozen all winter and summer. Pearson described his first look at the inside of it:

> It certainly was cold. About ten above, I'd judge. Beyond that fourth door I saw stacked up sides of caribou, moose, bear, skinned and cleaned rabbits, porcupines, ptarmigan—a whole year's supply of meat. All along one wall were shelves full of dozens of mouth-watering pies, cakes, bread, rolls, doughnuts— all frozen hard as rocks.

Fannie explained, "With this layout I can get all my game in the early fall, when it's at its best. And I can bake up pies and cakes and stuff whenever I have time on my hands. They freeze fast and taste just like fresh when you thaw 'em out."

Another tunnel with another series of doors was dug into gravel and thawed ground. This tunnel was kept cold but not frozen, and ensured fresh produce at any time of the year.

Joe was working the hard rock claims by that time, and lode mining had become more of his focus. With the respectability of marriage and a little bit of financial security, things were looking up and changing somewhat for Fannie. Her dream of a trip Outside to visit her sisters was finally realized in 1924, when she and Joe traveled to Washington and Oregon. They also visited Joe's family in Pennsylvania and Fannie's hometown of Wahoo, Nebraska. But Fannie was happy to return to her home on the mountain. The loneliness she had often felt in the past was dispelled as more women visited.

Mary Lee Davis, a well-known author of the time, once spent eleven days with Fannie at the cabin. Davis had come to Fairbanks with her husband and had fallen in love with Alaska. Endeavoring to explain the misunderstood northern territory to readers in the "lower 48," Davis had written a book, *Uncle Sam's Attic,* which attempted to describe the vast land of the last frontier. She followed that with *We Are Alaskans,* filled with stories of the amazing people she had met while living in Fairbanks. She devoted an entire chapter, complete with photographs, to Fannie and the time they had spent together.

Davis praised Fannie's skills as prospector, miner, hunter, trapper, naturalist, and self-taught scientist. There was apparently never a dull moment for a visitor of Fannie's. Davis wrote of waking to the sound of Fannie's stories and of sourdough pancakes sizzling on the "spider" iron skillet. "The last thing at night," Davis wrote, "I went to sleep with Fannie's epic tales still ringing in my ears."

One September day in 1926 Joe decided to catch a ride home from Fairbanks in a friend's plane. On landing, the plane overshot the sandbar on Moose Creek and when Fannie ran down after hearing the crash, there was Joe, with his nose "split down right in two, from right eye to his left tooth." Fannie further noted, "All I had was salt and iodine. But I sewed it up. I put in nine stitches." She later explained that she had used her "baseball stitch." Doctors in Fairbanks told her it shouldn't have been sewn that way, but she figured her stitches were as good as theirs, since it hadn't given Joe any more trouble.

In *A Mine of Her Own: Women Prospectors in the American West, 1850–1950,* Sally Zanjani writes:

> Fannie's sharp features, in a face with high cheekbones and dark frown, along with her petite stature, harsh tongue, and sulphurous cursing, developed over a lifetime of screeching at sled dogs, no doubt gave rise to her sobriquet "Little Witch of Denali."

In *We Are Alaskans,* Davis also commented on Fannie's speech, writing:

> Thank fortune, all the farness and the stillness haven't quieted Fannie's good gift of fervid vivid speech—dramatic, cogent, full of keen figurative language that is fairly Shakespearian in its rugged raciness.

The "rugged raciness" of Fannie's language was exemplified when she visited Ruth Campbell Barrack of Fairbanks. Mrs. Barrack and Mrs. Nan Robertson had spent two months at Quigley Ridge back in 1919 while they photographed Mt. McKinley. When Fannie came to Fairbanks she would "arrive unannounced and bang on the front door, never using the door bell, and yell, 'Kid, where the hell are you?' Dressed in men's clothing she looked rather witchlike and scared Ruth's daughters to death."

In 1930, Joe began working on a claim several miles from the house, and stayed there for several weeks at a time. Once a week Fannie carried over a supply of food. That May she arrived to find there had been a cave-in. She found Joe unconscious, with injuries to his hip and shoulder. After making him as comfortable as possible, she hiked 6 miles to find help, and eventually came across some miners, who helped her take Joe to Moose Creek. From there, a plane took him to the hospital in Fairbanks, where he was confined for several weeks. It was during this period that Fannie killed the two caribou in Moose Creek. Joe was later sent to Seattle for additional therapy on his shoulder. It was September before he returned home.

In December, Fannie wrote a letter to Mary Lee Davis, in which she described Joe's condition:

> They got his leg set three inches too long, and he can't put his
> arm up to his head. I have to rub his arm and leg an hour every
> night and morning, and do all work now, for he can't even cut
> wood. So everything is up to me. Joe is getting along very good.
> He walks about 8 miles every day.

But things were never the same between Fannie and Joe after the accident. In 1937 he sold his interest in the mines, and two years later, they divorced. Joe moved to Seattle and married a nurse he had met during his recovery there.

Fannie refused to leave Kantishna, and remained on the Friday Creek homestead. In telling stories of the past, she referred to times "when Joe was alive," possibly not willing to admit that he had left her. She continued to work her garden, and to kill, butcher, and dress out her own supply of wild game. She kept her tunnels stocked with more than enough meat, vegetables, and pastries to feed herself and the visitors who frequently stopped by her home.

She was almost seventy when Virgil Burford passed by the cabin, on his way to work a spot on Friday Creek. He found Fannie sitting at a table, drinking grain alcohol and water. She fed him cold caribou, homemade bread, blueberry pie, and hot coffee while she told him Kantishna mining stories.

In his book, *North to Danger,* Burford described her cabin:

The kitchen was small, most of one side was taken up by the plank table at which we sat. In a corner across the room there was a small porcelain sink with a drain through the plank floor. Gold pans sat about the walls, half-full of ore samples. A Yukon stove crouched against a far wall, throwing out a blaze of heat on this warm day. One wall was lined with plank shelves loaded with ore samples and rocks. A half-dozen rusty pickheads were stacked in a corner with a small anvil and hammer.

As Burford rose to leave, she spotted his pick and grabbed it from his pack. "How do you expect to work with tools like that?" she demanded, and proceeded to shove it into the stove and stir it around in the fire until the metal turned red. Then she took it over to the anvil and hammered it into a sharp point.

Handing it back to him, she explained, "There, at least you got one thing right now."

In 1940 she moved to a small white frame house near Moose Creek. There she lived by herself, preferring a solitary life. She continued to cuss vividly and drink heavily.

Her friend and neighbor, Johnny Busia, found her dead in her armchair one Friday in August of 1944, after he noticed that no smoke was coming from her smokestack. She was seventy-four years old.

Joe and Fannie Quigley are probably the best known of the Kantishna-area homesteaders, but it is Fannie who is remembered as a flamboyant, independent, yet accomplished character from Alaska's past. Rangers in Mt. McKinley National Park tell stories about her around campfires, and resorts entertain guests with programs that feature her. The little frame house where she lived out her life is open for visitors to the park in the summertime.

MARGARET KEENAN HARRAIS

1872–1964

Teacher, Humanitarian, Activist

IT WAS 1916 AND THE NEW SUPERINTENDENT of the Fairbanks schools was spending her first Christmas in Alaska on a trip to Nenana by dogsled. The "Malamute Kid," the musher she had hired to drive her, shouted unmentionable words to urge the dog team forward. The woman, who was wrapped warmly and securely in the sled, later wrote, "I, Margaret Keenan, spinster (good old common law term), knew that the Great Adventure was knocking at my door."

Nenana was a two-day journey away, and Margaret spent the night at a roadhouse in the company of fourteen men, sleeping in a space partitioned off for her with a thin muslin curtain. The visit in Nenana itself was pleasant, though uneventful, but the trip back to Fairbanks surely qualified as a "Great Adventure."

When the dogsled was still five hours from Chena, the overnight stop, an overfilled hot-water bottle burst and soaked Margaret's clothing and the wrappings in the sled. It was fifty degrees below zero and by the time they reached the roadhouse and saloon at Chena, she was covered with ice. It was only by the quick actions of the saloonkeeper's wife and Gertie, a woman of questionable reputation, that tragedy was averted. They carefully and slowly removed the frozen garments, warmed and fed Margaret, and dried her clothes so she could safely resume her journey the next day.

Margaret recalled, "I count every moment of the trip worthwhile, even the moment when the bag burst. The round-trip fare was $35.00, a bed was $1.00 and every meal was $1.50, and still it was worth it. You see, when I am an old-timer I can say, 'Why, yes, I was down that right of way long before the railroad was built.'"

Margaret Keenan was born in Batesville, Ohio, on September 23, 1872, the sixth child in a family of four girls and three boys. After graduating from Batesville High School in 1888, she immediately started on her long public education career. She taught in four different high schools in Ohio before finally attending Northern Indiana Normal School, where she received her teaching certificate.

From there Margaret went west, and became assistant principal of the high school in Dillon, Montana, and later, principal of a Challis, Idaho, high school. Her administrative skills must have been evident, for by 1901 she was elected superintendent of the Custer County, Idaho, school district. She remained there until 1906, when she returned to Indiana for more schooling at Valparaiso University.

In 1902 Margaret and her sister, Martha, took a two-week steamship trip to Skagway and back, so they could see Alaska. Although Margaret continued to work in Idaho for several more years, she continued to think about Alaska and, in 1914, made her way back to Skagway to become principal of the schools there. Two years later she moved farther north, became superintendent of the schools in Fairbanks, and experienced her ill-fated dogsled ride.

Margaret thrived in Fairbanks, and immediately began participating in and contributing to the life of the community. While in Idaho, she had been state president of the Woman's Christian Temperance Union (WCTU), so she sought out the local chapter of the

MARGARET HARRAIS WITH A MCCARTHY SCHOOLCHILD
AT MCCARTHY, ABOUT 1926

WCTU, and soon held the vice-president-at-large position for the state. She had arrived amidst the debate regarding an advisory vote to be held in November of 1916, for the prohibition of alcohol sales in the territory.

She worked tirelessly in conjunction with Dr. Aline Bradley and the Fairbanks women's group, the "Fourth Division Drys," to bring about the prohibition vote, which passed with more than a two-to-one margin. The result was sent to the U.S. Congress, and the "Bone Dry Law" was passed, prohibiting liquor traffic in Alaska two years before the 18th Amendment banned alcohol throughout the United States.

Margaret was incensed that public schools in Alaska had been supported with revenue from the liquor traffic. She was gratified when Congress, just before it adjourned, turned over to the territorial legislature the authority to maintain the schools. The Alaska Department of Education was created in 1917 and funding was guaranteed. In an interview for *The Union Signal,* the national newsletter of the WCTU, Margaret Keenan said, "For the first time in the history of Alaska, the education of the boys and girls of the territory will be carried on with clean, untainted money."

As the war raged overseas, the women in Fairbanks were asked to join coastal Alaskan women in raising the funds to provide one bed in the American Ambulance Hospital in Paris, at a cost of $600. To raise the money, Mrs. W. F. Thompson suggested that her husband's newspaper, *The Fairbanks Daily News-Miner,* put out a special women's edition. After much gruff opposition, her husband agreed, but only under the condition that Margaret Keenan be appointed editor-in-chief of the project. "While the others talk, talk, talk, Miss Keenan will get the job done," W. F. Thompson reportedly explained.

Starting at the end of September, Margaret taught school all day, then worked at the newspaper office every night, sometimes until two or three o'clock in the morning. She sought out the well-educated women of Fairbanks and encouraged their participation until she had enough articles for a forty-five-page paper. Then Thompson cut the edition to fifteen pages. Eventually, they reached a compromise, and Margaret was able to print almost all the articles she had planned, but only after a heated argument about what constituted "news" in a women's edition. The edition went on sale the night before Thanksgiving and raised enough money to sponsor not just one, but six beds in the American Ambulance Hospital.

Margaret also contributed to the war effort in other ways. She encouraged the children in the Fairbanks schools to participate in the Red Cross and Liberty Loan drives and even opened an employment office so the children could get jobs to raise funds. In the end, the students raised more than $16,000. Margaret herself set an example when she subscribed to the Fatherless Children of France program, and helped support two boys and two girls.

It was while she was in Fairbanks that Margaret met Martin Harrais. Friends in Seattle had spoken of him when she visited on her way to Skagway years earlier, and although she had not yet met him, she had often heard his name. Imagine her surprise to find that Martin was her neighbor across the hall in the building where she lived.

Martin Harrais was born in Russia and had made his own way in the world from the age of fourteen. He had sailed on Russian, British, and American ships, and worked in a California shipyard before moving to Seattle, where he eventually entered the University of Washington. After graduating in 1897, Martin joined the gold rush, struck it rich in the Yukon, and moved on to Fairbanks. He founded and invested in the town of Chena, and also had grandiose ideas of development in other nearby areas. These ideas failed to materialize, however, and when he met Margaret, he was struggling to reestablish his financial stability.

Although Margaret had not come to Alaska looking for a "big, strong, Sourdough," she could not help but be impressed by Martin. She described him as "tall, broad shouldered, muscular, with keen blue eyes, square jaw, sensitive lips and hands," and referred to him as "The Viking."

A relationship developed between Margaret and Martin, and they spoke of marriage. However, Martin did not want to marry until he had recouped his losses, and Margaret respected that. She had supported herself all of her life and had no qualms about doing so for a bit longer.

And, of course, there was the war. Martin had been unfairly accused of being pro-German. When it was announced that the president was calling for more men for overseas duty, and that there was a shortage of laborers in the shipbuilding and related trades, Martin Harrais wrote to the U.S. Civil Service Commission, high-lighting his many qualifications and offering his services. So in January of 1918, Margaret went Outside to accept a high school principal job in Shenandoah, Iowa, and Martin, at the age of fifty-three, volunteered for the war effort.

But Margaret was struck down in the influenza epidemic sweeping the country. She also developed pneumonia, recovered very slowly, and, at the suggestion of her doctors, traveled to several different spots seeking the right climate. In Colorado Springs, she was impressed by Pike's Peak, the inspiration for Katherine Lee Bates's poem, "America the Beautiful." She went on to Idaho and Oregon, before settling in San Diego, California, where she rented a small house.

By the fall of 1920, Martin was working for the Jumbo Mine at Kennecott. Since Margaret's doctor thought that she should not yet return to Alaska, Martin joined her in San Diego. Martin was fifty-five and Margaret was forty-eight when they were married on October 25, at the YMCA headquarters there. They spent the winter working on the little house and pursuing their individual writing projects. In the summer, Martin returned north to work.

Margaret wrote of that time:

> The next two years were spent in much the same fashion, delightful winters together in California and lonely, tho fruitful, summers separated. He searched and found what he considered another good mining property. I found strength in productive labor and the beauty in common things.

Finally, in the fall of 1924, with Martin working in the Nizina mining district, Margaret secured a teaching position in the nearby town of McCarthy. She boarded the Alaska steamship *Northwestern,* and looked around at the "friendly group of individualists, each one a distinct type right down to the soles of his feet," as she later wrote. "I said to myself, 'These are my people.' After six years absence I was going home!"

The trip was through the Inland Passage to Cordova, followed by a 192-mile train trip alongside the Copper River until they reached McCarthy, where, she noted, "Journeys end in lovers' meetings."

Martin had rented a three-room log cabin for the winter, and Margaret described the view from the kitchen window: "Mt. Blackburn, over 16,000 feet high is in plain view, and the woods are so full of Pike's Peaks that no one takes the trouble to name them."

The McCarthy school had just eleven students, but was remarkably supplied with everything that an up-to-date school should have. Margaret wasted no time in getting her students involved in helping the community, as well as learning their school lessons. They started with providing gift baskets for poorer families in an adjoining village. When the children wanted to do more, the wise teacher brought out a brochure about war orphans, and the children broadened their understanding of world geography by "adopting" an Armenian girl. They solicited funds from the miners, did odd jobs all over town to raise money, and proudly corresponded with the foreign child.

Margaret's work was again needed in the temperance cause. There was a move afoot to repeal the prohibition law. She took the position of WCTU president for Alaska, and convinced the Territorial Commissioner of Education to allow her to send materials to the territory's schoolteachers. But she didn't stop there. She sent literature to all Episcopalian and Presbyterian ministers in Alaska, and to the new president of the Federation of Women's Clubs. She also ordered *The Union Signal* to be sent to every newspaper in Alaska, to the new governor, and to William L. Paul, the native leader at Ketchikan.

Both measures regarding the repeal of prohibition that were proposed to the Alaska Legislature during the March 1925 session were defeated, primarily due to the work of the WCTU and Margaret Keenan Harrais.

The next few years in McCarthy were happy ones for Margaret, as she was able to work nearby or with her beloved Martin. In the summer of 1927, she accompanied him to his claim up the Chitina River. There, in a little log cabin between the majestic peaks of Mount St. Elias and Mt. Logan, they spent three glorious months together. They worked the claim, hiked the mountains and canyons, encountered a bear, and watched the mountain sheep. On the Fourth of July, they raised the colors, which consisted of a red bandanna, a white dishtowel, and the back of a blue shirt.

But soon the Great Depression caught up with them. As the price of copper fell, the mines slowed and families moved away. The McCarthy school closed in 1931, and Margaret taught the last two children in her home without pay. Their investments went sour and they again found themselves in financial straits. In 1932 Martin sold some supplies to the Kennecott Mine Company and bought the Sheep Bay Mill and Lumber Company in Cordova. At first Margaret helped out by doing the bookkeeping and by cooking for the men, but in the fall she accepted a teaching position at Ellamar, a small, almost deserted town halfway between Cordova and Valdez. There she moved into a two-room combination residence and classroom and taught eight native children.

In 1936 Martin was appointed United States Commissioner in Valdez and bought a six-room frame house there. Margaret took a teaching job at Fort Liscum, which was a scant 4 miles from Valdez, but as it was across the water, she lived there. She reached the required retirement age, but asked the Commissioner of Education to allow her to continue because "Mr. Harrais, as Commissioner at Valdez, is not paid enough to buy us a home and social security for old age." Commissioners in Alaska were not guaranteed a salary, but rather paid on a fee system, which brought in very little money. Margaret was granted another year of teaching.

In mid-December Margaret received word that Martin was very ill. It was several days before the weather allowed her to cross the water, and when she did, she found that he had been taken to the hospital in Seward. Conditions would not allow flying, so Margaret waited, miserably.

She wrote, "The storm abated and I was putting on my wraps for the air flight, when the message came that the light of my life had gone out the evening before—Christmas Day, 1936, at five o'clock."

After finishing that teaching year, Margaret moved into the frame house in Valdez and took over the position of U.S. Commissioner. She had worried about what would "tie her to the other members of the human family" when she stopped teaching and no longer had daily contact with students. She found her answer in the courts:

I have acquired an amazing family composed of the down-and-outs, derelicts and unfortunates. My "family" is not as attractive as a group of clean, eager-eyed children; but neither am I as attractive as a young, eager-eyed teacher, so, maybe there is a sense of fitness in the situation. Each generation must solve its own problems, and I am helping to solve the problems of mine.

Margaret had often paraphrased, "And now abideth faith, hope, and charity; but the greatest of these is a sense of humor!"

And she certainly needed a sense of humor when she began sending the manuscript of her book to publishers. For several years she had been writing the story of her life in Alaska, titling the work, *Alaska Periscope*. After typing it and keeping one carbon copy, she sent the original off to New York in 1943. At least one editor replied with interest, but wanted an opening chapter about her earlier life, wanted her to "insert herself" more into the story, and wanted to change the title. After several letters and suggestions back and forth, the manuscript was rejected. Margaret told the company not to return it to Alaska, that she would let them know what to do with it. Finally a niece, who was a "literary major" college graduate, retrieved the manuscript and criticized it heavily, so Margaret told her to send it back. Unfortunately, the ship on which it was returning to Alaska sank.

Margaret painstakingly recreated it from the carbon copy, changing and improving it as she went along. Nevertheless, she still failed to find a publisher, and the manuscript was filed away. (It is now preserved in the archives of the Rasmuson Library, at the University of Alaska in Fairbanks.)

Margaret continued to serve the community in many ways. When the population was called upon once again to support the war effort, Margaret declared her willingness "to keep open house, a full cookie jar for the soldiers, to patch my dresses, darn my stockings and redarn the darns . . . and buy war bonds."

She remained president of the Alaska WCTU until 1942, and was the only member-at-large of the League of Women Voters in Alaska. She actively campaigned for Alaska statehood and used her letter-writing skills in correspondence with B. W. Thoron, the director of the Division of Territories and Island Possessions.

Margaret remained in her position as Commissioner until Alaska became a state in 1959, at which time she became a deputy magistrate for the state court system. She served in that capacity until her retirement on September 4, 1962, at the age of ninety.

The white frame house in Valdez, which had served as court for so many years, was washed away in the Good Friday earthquake and tidal wave of 1964. Margaret was evacuated to Glennallen, where she developed pneumonia and died at the hospital there on April 26.

Margaret Keenan Harrais loved the state of Alaska and sought to make life better for those who lived there. She worked through both one-on-one contacts with individuals and through campaigns for better laws.

When she retired as deputy magistrate, the "Tribute to an Alaska Lady, Margaret Keenan Harrais, of Valdez," that Senator E. L. "Bob" Bartlett read into the *Congressional Record* noted, in part, "Her life has been a model of all that is good and decent and constructive."

NELLIE NEAL LAWING

1873-1956

The Legendary "Alaska Nellie"

A SMALL, WIRY WOMAN WITH CURLY GRAY HAIR hurried over to the tourists who were scrambling off the train.

"Welcome to Lawing, at Mile 23," she called. "How was your boat trip? What do you think of Alaska? Come on, I know you want to see my museum, and we don't have all day!"

The group followed as the woman walked briskly down a path that led to an old two-story cabin on the bank of Kenai Lake. Entering the large room, the travelers gasped with amazement at the array of Alaskan wildlife displayed on every wall and in every corner.

"Alaska Nellie" began telling her stories. "Yep, I killed 'em all myself," she proudly announced. "That big brown bear? My pet bear, Mike, was lost, and I went running into the woods to find him. 'Round a bend was the biggest, meanest bear I ever saw, standing over poor little Mike's dead body! I turned and ran for home, but he followed me and I just barely got the barn door open in time to run in and pull it behind me—but he slammed into it and scratched my arm and broke my three fingers and bruised my knee, see. . . ."

She pulled back her sleeve and showed the crowd her scars. "Then I waited 'til it got real quiet, slipped into the house, got my gun, and went after him. I saw him on the ridge the same time he saw me. He reared up and I sent a bullet into him, hit him in the foot, then another hit him in the leg. Had to shoot him six times 'fore he keeled over!"

It was a good story, and it got better every time she told it. She could have told a similarly exciting tale about any item in the room.

Nellie Trosper was born in Missouri, on July 25, 1873, the eldest of ten surviving children. As a child, she fished, hunted, trapped, and did farm work alongside her brothers. She dreamed of going to Alaska to hunt moose and bear, and often told her parents she would live there one day and drive a dog-sled team.

Nellie left school before she was fourteen to help her mother with the family. Although she worked away from home for a short time in Missouri, she returned when her mother grew ill. After her mother died, she stayed on to help until her father remarried. Finally, at the age of twenty-seven, Nellie left home for good.

Her journey to Alaska had many twists and turns along the way. She worked at railroad restaurants in Wyoming and Colorado, before beginning work at a boarding house in Cripple Creek, Colorado. Eventually, she ran a boarding house of her own there. She met and married Wesley Neal, a mine assayer, but after a short time of happiness, the marriage began to disintegrate.

"My home life was made unbearable by that demon, rum, which destroys the best in man," wrote Nellie. She left her husband, and Cripple Creek, to continue the westward journey that would lead her, at last, to Alaska.

It was July 3, 1915, when Nellie Neal arrived in the land of her heart's desire. She was forty-two years old. As she sat in her hotel room in Seward that night, she penned this poem:

After many solemn years had fled,

By an unseen force I had been led

To the land of my sweet childhood dreams,

Where the midnight sun on the ocean gleams.

With her boarding-house experience, she soon found work at the Kenai Gold Mine, where she was hired to cook and drive the freight wagon. When the train stopped to unload supplies at Roosevelt, on the edge of Kenai Lake, she was delighted with what she saw. Writing about it later, she recalled, "This place seemed very familiar to me and I hoped that I might some day come back here and make my home."

Nellie's childhood hunting and trapping skills came in handy, as she was often able to secure fresh meat for the hungry miners. On one of her trips into the wilderness, she came upon an abandoned miner's cabin and a plan began to form in her mind. When the mine crew stopped work and moved into Seward for the winter, Nellie had other ideas.

In Seward she purchased a sled and supplies, and then, very early on a crisp December morning, she set out from Seward, following the railroad track. As she had no dogs, she "necked" the sled—that is, pulled it herself, by way of a strap around her shoulders. After traveling for 23 miles, she came to Roosevelt and spent the night with the roadhouse proprietors, Mr. and Mrs. Roberts. The next day she covered the remaining 7 miles, using snowshoes for the first time in her life. She arrived at the little abandoned miner's cabin where she would spend the winter and began to make her new quarters hospitable. In writing about this experience, Nellie quipped, "If one has never tried cutting wood while on snowshoes, he should really try it as a new outdoor sport."

For the next three months, Nellie ran trap lines, prepared the collected pelts from rabbit, fox, ermine, mink, and lynx, and developed plans for her future. On a clear, cold Christmas Eve, she was

ALASKA NELLIE IN HER TROPHY ROOM

awestruck at first experiencing the shimmering, glowing curtain of colors that were the Northern Lights.

When Nellie returned to Seward in the spring of 1916, the U.S. government had purchased the Alaska Railroad and planned to extend the tracks from Seward to Anchorage. Nellie applied to run an eating house on the construction line and was awarded a contract for the roadhouse at Mile 45—she was the first woman to be so selected.

The contract provided that she would be allowed to purchase supplies from the government commissary, have free freight by rail, be paid 50 cents per meal, and charge $1.00 per night for lodging. She would collect vouchers from the employees and turn them in each month for payment.

So Nellie set up business at Mile 45, renaming the roadhouse there "Grandview." Ever resourceful, she made a sign for the building using blue letters cut from an old coat and sewn onto white canvas. She assumed there would be ample business opportunities for at least three years.

At that time, the train from Seward came to Mile 40, at Hunter. From there the mail and other supplies had to come by wagon in summer and by dog team in winter. Nellie knew she would need kennels and a cookhouse for dog food, so she proceeded to cut trees and saw them into logs for the buildings. By the time winter arrived, the kennels were ready. She acquired a dog team for her sled and became an expert musher.

Soon Nellie could traverse the 45-mile trip from Grandview to Seward on snowshoes in a day, and had braved many a heavy blizzard with her dog team and sled. Stories about her prowess on the trail began to circulate, and her exploits were touted around roadhouse kitchens all over the territory. But it was during her second Alaska winter that the stories about Nellie began to take on legend status.

By then the track had been extended past Grandview for several miles. In November she heard that the train was stuck over the summit in a snowstorm two miles away at Mile 47.

"Every available man has been sent here to help dig us out, and there are at least fifty men here now who have been working feverishly since early morning and without food," the roadmaster told her by telephone. He had attached his portable unit to a telephone line to make the call.

When the train failed to arrive after several hours, Nellie began cooking ham and eggs for sandwiches, frying doughnuts, and making coffee until she had enough for fifty men. She packed it in a washtub, loaded it on her sled, and set out through the storm. When she reached the train, the men were exhausted and hungry. The food gave them the energy they needed to finish digging out the train, which finally returned to Grandview, taking eighteen hours to travel seven miles. There would be no more trains over the summit until spring.

On January 20, 1917, a day that the mail was to come by dog team from Tunnel to Grandview and then on to meet the train at

Hunter, there came a wild blowing snowstorm. By two o'clock it was totally dark, and the carrier had not yet arrived at Grandview. Nellie contacted Tunnel and was told the carrier had left five hours earlier. After waiting another five hours, Nellie knew something was wrong. She donned her parka, hitched her dogs to the sled, threw in a rabbit-skin robe, shovel, lantern, and snowshoes, and was on her way to the rescue.

With the snow swirling around her, Nellie made her way along the railroad track, sometimes having to put on her snowshoes and travel in front of the dogs to break the trail through the snow, or shovel their way through a huge snowdrift. At last, the dogs plunged up and over the last drift to where they found the carrier's dogs and the carrier, huddled in his sled, nearly frozen. She helped the man onto her sled and struggled to rouse the dogs from where they had bedded themselves down in the snow.

When she reached Grandview, she nursed the carrier's near-frozen hands, feet, and face, provided him with hot drinks, and settled him to sleep. Then Nellie returned to the mail sled, hitched her dogs to it, and trailed her own sled behind it. When she got back to Grandview and saw that her "patient" was still sleeping, she decided to take the mail on to its next delivery stop at Hunter. By the time she returned to Grandview, it was seven o'clock in the morning!

The next Christmas, Nellie received a great surprise. As a reward for her valiant rescue, a group of pioneers in Seward sent her a necklace of solid gold nuggets, with a larger nugget pendant set with a diamond. The accompanying note read:

To Nellie—from oldtimers
Who on snowshoes broke down the trail;
Who fought the elements to take through the mail.
They struggled on without food or rest—
To rescue the perishing they did their best.

The necklace was her most prized possession and she wore it the rest of her life.

Two years had seen the extension of track so that the Alaska Railroad now reached from Seward to Kern Creek, 26 miles north of Grandview. Nellie purchased the roadhouse at Kern Creek, overlooking Turnagain Arm, and when hunting season came, she started on her collection of Alaska wildlife trophies. The first moose she killed had thirty-eight-point antlers with a sixty-eight-inch spread. She took down two mountain sheep in one day, and her first bear had a hide measuring 7 feet from nose to tail. It was at Kern Creek that she had her little pet bear, Mike. Nellie's encounter with the big brown bear that killed him gave her ample storytelling material for many years.

After her three-year contract with the railroad ended, and after an unsuccessful foray into the mining business, Nellie found herself again running a roadhouse. She managed to procure another contract, this one at Dead Horse Hill, or Mile 248, halfway between Seward and Fairbanks. She saw it as another good opportunity, and anticipated a need for the housing and feeding of workers for some time to come.

In the winter of 1922, Nellie and one of the construction workers became sweethearts. Kenneth Holden had come to Alaska from Seattle. His mother and his cousin, Billie Lawing, remained there, waiting for him to send for them once he was settled. Kenneth was charming and witty, and he played the piano and sang beautifully. He and Nellie became engaged the night before he went off on a construction job. He entertained at a party that night, and his last songs were "Somewhere a Voice is Calling," and "The End of a Perfect Day." Kenneth died in an accident on that job, and Nellie was heartbroken. She bought the piano on which he had played his final melodies and traveled to Seward with his coffin, which was put on a ship to Seattle. His mother died soon after, and his cousin began a correspondence with Nellie.

In July of 1923, President Warren G. Harding traveled to Alaska to drive in the Golden Stake signifying the completion of the Alaska Railroad. His entourage, including his wife and Herbert Hoover, stopped overnight at Dead Horse Hill. Harding wanted to meet "Nellie Neal," whose signature had graced those expense vouchers sent to Washington, D.C. It was chilly when morning came around, so Nellie served breakfast on the table in the warm kitchen. When she noted an expression of disapproval from one of the guests, she said, frankly, "Presidents of the United States like to be comfortable when they eat, just like anybody else." The president and the secretary agreed wholeheartedly.

With the completion of the Alaska Railroad came the expiration of Nellie's Dead Horse Hill contract. She was looking for a new project when she received a letter that offered the fulfillment of her dream. Mrs. Roberts, from Roosevelt, the beautiful spot on Kenai Lake with which Nellie had been so taken years earlier, was willing to sell her property. Mr. Roberts had died and she wanted to return to the States. Nellie was on the next train to meet her and sign the papers.

The log building was perfect for Nellie's long-desired trophy room. Her collection by now included dozens of moose, bear, sheep, and other game, as well as a number of birds. She spent hours arranging the displays as she had always seen them in her mind.

Shortly after her arrival at Roosevelt, she received a letter from Billie Lawing in Seattle. Having lost both his cousin and his aunt, he was particularly lonely. He wanted to come to Alaska and marry Nellie. She, too, was feeling the need for companionship, and so she agreed to marry him. They met in Seward and were wed on the stage of the Seward Theatre on September 8, 1923, right after the show.

About their return to Roosevelt, Nellie wrote, "When Billie entered the trophy room, he was speechless with surprise."

Nellie was now truly living her childhood dream. She and Billie renamed the location Lawing, and Nellie was appointed postmistress. They made many improvements to their property, and soon Lawing was a recreation destination for Seward residents, as well as tourists. The twice-weekly train stopped for ten minutes so that Nellie could take visitors through her "Wildlife Museum." On Kenai Lake, Billie operated a 36-foot cabin cruiser, christened the *Nellie Neal*. For thirteen years their idyllic spot on the edge of the lake gave them joy. Then in March of 1936, Nellie's Billie died of heart failure while cutting ice from the lake.

Nellie continued to entertain tourists, both long-term cabin guests and ten-minute train visitors. Her extensive garden provided fresh vegetables even early in the season, since she started the seedlings in a hothouse. To provide fresh fish for the table, Nellie rigged a line that dropped right out her kitchen window into the lake. It was attached to a bell so that when a fish took the hook, the line pulled on the bell and Nellie knew dinner was on the other end. Many celebrities stayed at Lawing, including silent film star, Alice Calhoun, who became a good friend.

In 1938, Nellie finished the autobiography she had started years earlier and took the manuscript by bus to New York City, in search of a publisher. On her trip she personally presented four Alaska potatoes to President Franklin D. Roosevelt. Her return trip took her to California, where she visited Alice Calhoun. Alice found someone to help Nellie "polish up" her manuscript.

In 1940, MGM released a short documentary on Nellie, calling it "In the Land of Alaska Nellie," and her famous nickname was born. That same year Seattle's Chieftain Press published her book, *Alaska Nellie*. On a book tour across the country, she attended President Roosevelt's third inauguration as a special guest. She was a shameless self-promoter and sold hundreds of copies of her book to the public on book tours, to tourists who stopped at Lawing, and to soldiers whom she entertained with stories at the Seward USO. Most of the copies sold by her were autographed, "Sincerely, Alaska Nellie."

Nellie lived the rest of her life in Lawing. The trains slowed their service from Seward in the late 1940s. Still, tourists, coming by bus and automobile, continued to visit Alaska Nellie's famous wildlife museum. As the buildings fell into disrepair, there were fewer overnight guests, but Nellie continued to provide excellent home-cooked meals. She invited neighbors and trappers to join her for Christmas, with colored lights blazing on trees in the snow, and a great feast.

One old-timer remembered:

> There were all kinds of roasts—bear, moose, caribou, reindeer. There were vegetables, cakes, pies—even hardtack for the Swedes. We joked and told stories while we ate and drank until we could hold no more. Then came the dance with the old phonograph wheezing out "Bye Bye Blackbird" and "Roll Out the Barrel." Nellie was my partner most of the time. She was tall and slim and danced like a bird. She was in her sixties but only looked about twenty-three.

On January 21, 1956, Nellie was honored in Anchorage with "Alaska Nellie Day." Scarcely four months later, she died at home in Lawing, on May 10, at the age of eighty-two.

Nellie Trosper Neal Lawing came to Alaska and became a legend. She was known for her exploits and storytelling, and in 1942 a letter addressed only to "Nellie, Alaska," was delivered to her promptly. Her life personified the independent, able-bodied, and sometimes outrageous spirit of the pioneers who helped build Alaska.

LOIS HUDSON ALLEN

1873–1948

Journalist with a Purpose

LOIS HUDSON ALLEN STOOD ON THE DECK OF THE SHIP as it steamed its way toward Skagway. She pulled her heavy coat around her shoulders and tugged her wool scarf tighter over her ears, bracing against the cold Alaska wind. The lengthy dawn had painted the sky a brilliant pink, and the sun was finally beginning to peek over the snow-capped mountains. In the distance ahead she could see the buildings and piers that were her destination. What kind of welcome awaited her there? Had she made the right decision?

It had been almost a year since Lois had waited in her doctor's office in Colorado Springs and been given the devastating diagnosis of breast cancer. Independent as always, she kept the news to herself and began to plan ways to take charge of her illness and do something important with the rest of her life. She would leave Colorado and not be a burden to her two sons, who were starting families of their own.

She had read about Alaska—the Last Frontier! Surely there would be a need there for her expertise in journalism. Going right to the top, she wrote to the territorial governor, John Weir Troy, in

Juneau, and asked him what town most needed a newspaper. His response was Skagway.

Now the ship had docked and Lois watched as the cargo was unloaded.

"What will they think of me?" she thought to herself. "Just an eccentric old lady? Well, they don't have to know how old . . . perhaps I'll just subtract five years. If anyone has the nerve to ask, I'll say I'm only fifty-eight!"

Resolutely, Lois Allen strode down the gangplank to where her typewriter and mimeograph machine awaited her. It was fall 1936.

Lois Hudson Allen was born in Fredonia, Kansas, in 1873, the first child of Thomas Jefferson Hudson and Emma Rosella Campbell Hudson. Her father was an outspoken Democrat and, at one point, was political editor for the local newspaper. He was also the county attorney and a successful banker, as well as a cattle rancher. He went on to represent Kansas as a U.S. senator. Lois's mother had graduated in the first class from Washburn College in Topeka, Kansas.

It was natural that Lois, with her family background, was also well educated and politically minded. She attended Baker University in Baldwin City, Kansas, and then graduated from St. Mary's Academy of Notre Dame in South Bend, Indiana.

In 1892, when her father started his two-year senate term in Washington, D.C., nineteen-year-old Lois went with him as his secretary. There, she had ample opportunity to witness the inner workings of the political arena and, no doubt, noticed that there were no female faces in either the House or the Senate. Her time in Washington also impressed upon her the importance of the written word to the public and elected officials and, quite possibly, sowed the seed for her later endeavors.

When her father, though renominated in 1894, declined to run for a second senate term, Lois returned to Kansas with him. Within a year she married Guy Wiley Allen, a cashier in her father's bank.

Lois was delighted with Colorado, especially Manitou Springs and Colorado Springs, where the couple traveled on their honeymoon. After visiting relatives and friends there, they returned to make their home in Fredonia. Over the course of the next twelve years, Lois and Guy had three sons, Hudson, James, and Frank.

Lois, as wife and mother, was settling into a comfortable life in Fredonia when her husband died suddenly of an undisclosed illness in 1908. She was left with three young boys and another on the way. Andrew was born shortly after his father's death.

Lois could have continued to live in Fredonia, surrounded by family and the financial security they offered her. But she was a woman of fierce independence, and she packed up her four sons and moved with them to Colorado Springs.

Lois knew there were few opportunities available for women in the professional arena. She declined to enter into the teaching or nursing fields, but ardently desired to do something that would make a difference in society. She chose journalism.

According to family lore, Lois approached the owner of the daily *Colorado Springs Telegraph* and requested a job as a reporter, but was refused because she was a woman. Undaunted, she continued to show up at the office every day and wrote stories as if she were working there. Finally, on the basis of her reporting skills—and, no doubt, her persistence—she was hired.

In 1915, Lois purchased the weekly *Manitou Springs Journal*. Manitou Springs was a little mountain village, which attracted seasonal tourists to its hot springs and mineral waters. The following year she tried to convert the publication to a daily, but the community couldn't support the change, and so Lois sold the business.

For the next several years, Lois published the *Fremont County Leader* in Canon City, Colorado. Her youngest son, Andrew, died in the flu epidemic of 1918, but her three older sons helped in the newspaper office and learned the printing trade.

LOIS HUDSON ALLEN STANDING OUTSIDE HER HOUSE IN MOOSE PASS

In 1920, her fellow newspaper professionals honored Lois by electing her president of the Colorado Press Association. The next year Lois shut down the Canon City paper and moved with her sons to Pueblo, Colorado, where she operated the Allen Printing Company. Her son, Frank, died in 1930; Hudson and James subsequently moved to Denver.

Lois then moved back to Colorado Springs and published the *Colorado Springs Independent* weekly for a year, followed by the *Colorado Springs Shopping News.*

And it was in 1935 when she was diagnosed with breast cancer.

The United States was still in the throes of the Great Depression. Jobs were hard to find and men all over the country were reduced to performing whatever menial tasks they could find in order to feed their children. President Franklin D. Roosevelt had initiated his "New Deal," a domestic program designed for economic recovery. As a part of this program, 203 poverty-stricken families from Minnesota, Wisconsin, and Michigan were selected to travel to Alaska and start new farms in the fertile Matanuska Valley, north of Anchorage.

There was quite a bit of publicity about the "Matanuska Colonists," as they were known, and Alaska was touted as a great land with infinite possibilities. Lois, a life-long Democrat, undoubtedly approved of FDR's "New Deal," and the prospect of adventure in Alaska would have appealed to her, as she sought an appropriate destination for her new life on her own. She was obviously impressed with the Matanuska Colonists, as was apparent in the 1940 article she wrote for *Alaska Sportsman* magazine, in which she documented the colonists' progress and accomplishments.

So Lois followed the advice she had received from Governor Troy and by the fall of 1936, she was in Skagway. Whether or not she had known of Governor Troy's publishing background, asking his advice proved to be serendipitous. Although he was publisher of the *Daily Alaska Empire* in Juneau before becoming governor, he had published a newspaper in Skagway for many years before moving to the capital city. Coming to Skagway with his blessing certainly made it easier for her to begin her business. Lois was grateful for his support and returned the favor with many favorable mentions of him in her paper. She also wrote a complimentary article in the *Alaska Sportsman* in 1939, as he prepared to retire from the governor's office.

The Skagway that Lois Allen found when she arrived was a far cry from the boomtown of the Klondike Gold Rush days. The population was a slight 500, and the town itself was a mere four blocks wide. Skagway sought to find a role for itself in the Alaska economy and it looked as if the fledgling tourist business might be the answer to its financial woes. Even the small weekly newspaper that Lois established was a welcome asset to a town that had been without a regular publication for several years.

Although she would have to do without her beloved printing press and linotype, Lois had every confidence that her typewriter and mimeograph machine would serve her purposes splendidly. She approached this challenge in her life just as she had others, with verve and a sense of great adventure. Because the typewriter limited her size and style of type, Lois used handwritten and printed letters and numerals for such things as advertisements and the eye-catching masthead. She even drew occasional freehand images for some of the advertisers. This gave the newspaper pages a bold and interesting look.

Lois named her new publication after the word that, in Alaska, means "newcomer." Of course, it only emphasized what a newcomer she was when, for the first three issues, she misspelled the word! Those first three issues were titled the *Skagway Chechako*. After that the correction was made and Lois's newspaper became the *Skagway Cheechako*.

Lois gathered material for the newspaper in many ways. She had access to the telegraph system and radio, as well as news and stories brought into Skagway by passengers on the ships that docked there. She strove to put into each issue important news from around the world, both noteworthy political information and trivial but interesting items. She and her readers followed closely the story about the missing aviatrix, Amelia Earhart. She often noted such gossip as "Jeannette MacDonald was married to Gene Raymond Thursday at her home in Hollywood," as if celebrities were just regular town folks. And the important "shipping news" was always published so that everyone would know not only which ships were coming and going, but who was coming and going on them.

Lois also knew that one of the secrets of getting the public to read her newspaper was to be sure that Skagway residents found their own names mentioned in it. So every issue contained articles about such events as the local sewing club meetings—who the hostess was, who attended, and what delicious tidbit was served. Harriet Pullen's Pullen House Hotel was also frequently mentioned, noting who entertained whom and for what reason, who was staying there, and what Mrs. Pullen was doing that week!

Publishing a newspaper written on a typewriter was not without its unique difficulties. Once, Lois's typewriter broke down and she had to use a borrowed one. She explained the change of typeface by noting that the "office typewriter usually employed by the *Cheechako* decided to 'quit' (and a new one was hired)."

One most interesting issue appeared that was completely handwritten. It began with this paragraph:

Not being able to rent or steal a typewriter in Skagway we are doing the next best thing. We have bought a new typewriter which can be here on the 27th but probably won't. When the insurance company finds our typewriter which was sent outside for repair early in the summer, we'll have two typewriters and won't we be rich—in typewriters?

After about a year and a half in Skagway, Lois decided on a move. The newspaper of May 27, 1938, bid farewell to the town:

AU REVOIR BUT NOT GOOD-BYE: With this issue the *Cheechako* dies with its boots on, i.e.—with all bills paid. The editah of the papah is off to the Westward for the same reason that the bear came over the mountain. If she (the editah not the bear) sees any place that suits her better than Skagway, she'll be surprised.

Although living in Skagway had been a good experience for Lois, the town was separated from the outside world and her readership was limited. She still preferred a small community, but wanted to be in a location where she could influence a larger population. Given her health condition, she probably also wanted to be closer to medical resources.

So Lois moved to Moose Pass, a small mountain community between Seward and Anchorage. Although fewer than one hundred people actually resided in the town, it was connected by roads a few miles south to Lawing, a small resort on Kenai Lake; north to Cooper's Landing on the other side of the lake; and to Hope, on Turnagain Arm. It was also connected to Seward and Anchorage by rail.

Lois bought a small house next to the post office. Armed with her trusty typewriter and mimeograph machine, she again launched into the newspaper business. The *Moose Pass Miner*, "devoted to the interests of Moose Pass and the Kenai Peninsula," was born in January of 1939.

The *Miner* contained the same kinds of articles that had appeared in her Skagway paper: bits of gossip about local residents' comings and goings, notices of social events and recreational items, and, of course, the attendees and menus for the weekly meetings of the local sewing club. Here Lois became more involved with the community. She joined the sewing club, and when she had her turn as hostess, she referred to herself not as L. H. Allen, as it said on the newspaper masthead, but as "Mrs. Lois H. Allen," who served "veal in aspic, toasted crackers, coffee and tea."

But now Lois was more knowledgeable about her adopted state, and the newspaper began to carry editorials about what she believed was important for the future of Alaska. The *Miner* advocated more roads in Alaska. Lois agreed wholeheartedly with Anthony J. Dimond, Alaska's delegate to the U.S. Congress, and wrote:

> Airfields and roads were named by the Delegate as the two most important needs of Alaska, and among the road needs of the Territory he placed particular emphasis on a road to connect the Richardson Highway with the Matanuska Valley, and a road to open up Kenai Peninsula from Cooper's Landing to Homer by way of Kenai.

Her editorials also suggested that many more people could and should move to Alaska, and that those who were already living here should be more welcoming to newcomers. "Alaska needs people!" she wrote.

By this time, Lois was discovering that running a small weekly newspaper was not adequate to pay the bills. She started selling a few stationery supplies from her home and also rented out her secretarial skills. Primarily, though, she wrote several articles for the *Alaska Sportsman*. Besides penning "Sourdough Governor," about Governor Troy, and "Matanuska Gets Down to Business," she highlighted Martin Itjen, who ran a streetcar tour of Skagway, in "He

Takes 'Em for a Ride." She also featured Moose Pass fur farmer Russell Williams in two articles and reported on some of the amazing adventures of her neighbor, Nellie Neal Lawing, in "Woman Unafraid."

By this time in 1942, the military presence was growing in Alaska. The readership in Moose Pass was shrinking, as residents moved to Seward or Anchorage to work in war-related jobs. Unwilling to sacrifice her small-town living, Lois responded to the call for teachers and took a position teaching in the two-classroom Ninilchik Territorial School, south of Kenai. Of course she took her typewriter and mimeograph machine with her and helped her eighth-grade students produce Ninilchik's only newspaper. Ninilchik was accessible only by plane or boat. During the year she lived there, Lois visited Homer, where a mimeographed newspaper had recently been started, and also traveled to Kenai and Kasilof. The idea about her next project must have come about at this time, as she began taking photographs of the areas she visited.

After one year of teaching, Lois retired and moved to Hope. While in Moose Pass, she had visited Hope and been extremely impressed with the area. In fact, she had written in the *Miner*:

> Having seen Hope, it won't be necessary for us to see the Garden of Eden. Lovely, peaceful, historic Hope! Such gardens!

and:

> It may not have been ladylike—in fact we are practically certain it wasn't—but after seeing the Hope gardens, the editor came home and kicked her garden.

Lois decided to write a book about the Kenai Peninsula. She believed that Alaska would soon be at the forefront of the tourist industry and wanted her beloved Kenai Peninsula to benefit from it. So she began to describe all the wonderful places she had visited and wrote glowing reports, designed to bring tourists by the droves, adding wonderful photographs taken by herself and others.

By the summer of 1946, she had completed her manuscript and sent it to a printer in Denver. She ordered 400 copies and sent him a check for $275. Unfortunately, the books didn't arrive in time to be sold for Christmas that year, but Lois advertised them in the *Alaska Sportsman* the following spring. She sold them at newsstands all over the Peninsula and at the Alaska Shop in Seward. Lois's book, *Alaska's Kenai Peninsula,* was the first guide to the now extremely popular tourist destination.

By the following year Lois's health was deteriorating rapidly. Her next-door neighbor, Emma Clark, was a certified nurse and cared for Lois during this time. Finally, after thirteen years of battling her illness, Lois Allen succumbed to her breast cancer at the Seward Hospital on July 20, 1948. She was seventy-four years old. Both her obituary and her gravestone list the wrong birth date, reflecting the five years that she had subtracted on coming to Alaska.

Although Lois Hudson Allen spent only the last thirteen years of her life in Alaska, she contributed much to her adopted state. Her independence and courage were examples to the women and girls she met along the way. Her intellect and humor, which she brought to all of the communities in which she lived, were greatly appreciated, as was the valuable information she supplied to her readers. She was one of the first people to appreciate the impact that the tourist industry could have on the economics of the Kenai Peninsula, and would have been gratified to know that her book did, indeed, contribute to tourism in the area.

JOSEPHINE SATHER

1882-1964

Fox Farmer and Nature Lover

JOSEPHINE ROWED HER SMALL SKIFF UP TO THE SHORE, bringing fresh fish and cooked sea lion meat for the fox-feeding station there. One of the terrible Nuka Bay downpours had just abated, leaving little streams of water flowing down the banks and into the sea. She pulled the craft onto the sand and began unloading her supplies when she heard an unusual sound coming from the hillside.

There was an old fox den a couple of hundred feet above the beach, where the same pair of foxes had lived for eight or nine years. A spring of clear water was located about 50 feet from the den and the powerful rains had washed down a mass of loose dirt and debris, clogging up the spring's outlet. Now the water was backing up and had almost reached the nest in the den. The mother fox was frantically digging, sending dirt flying down the hill.

Normally, when the fox heard Josephine coming in the skiff, she would come down from her den and wait leisurely for the food's arrival. Josephine called to her, but the fox didn't even look up. When Josephine hurried up the hillside and saw the dirt piled in front of the entrance, she understood—the babies were in danger of being drowned and the mother fox was doing everything she could to save them. She was digging a ditch to carry the water off the outer edge of the pile!

"What can I use to help this poor mother?" Josephine thought. She went back to the skiff to see if she had anything that would do; her eyes fell on the skiff anchor. She quickly unlashed it, tied the skiff to a driftwood log, scrambled back up the hillside, and joined in the digging. As Josephine took over, the mother fox walked away and lay down, exhausted and weary with anxiety. The anchor turned out to be the perfect tool for hoeing out the dirt. As the water drained away, the mother fox slid back down into the nest.

The next time Josephine delivered to that feeding station, she checked on the fox den and saw that the mother fox had dug a new outlet for the spring, allowing for better drainage. Although the downpours had come every day since Josephine had hoed with the anchor, the area around the nest was dry. She knew that the young foxes were safe.

Josephine Sather lived for forty years on Nuka Island, a remote spot 8 miles long and 4 miles wide, off the southeast coast of the Kenai Peninsula. She spent many hours observing the habits of the numerous species of wildlife that abounded there, as well as the foxes that had been introduced to the island and which supplied her livelihood.

Josephine Maier was born in Ellmau, Austria, in 1882, and grew up surrounded by the grandeur of the Tyrolean Alps. At the age of nineteen, she married Balthauser Angerman. With their young son, Frank, the Angermans emigrated to America in 1911, settling first in Massachusetts. Disenchanted with the cotton mills environment, they headed across the continent and ended up in Kennicott, Alaska. In 1915 the Angermans' marriage was annulled. Five years later Josephine married Edward Tuerck and was living in Cordova.

JOSEPHINE SATHER

In 1920, a flurry of excitement spread through Cordova when the price for blue fox skins reached up to $120 each. When two former residents sold the furs from their island farm for $17,000, Josephine and Edward were impressed. The following spring, Edward set out to find the perfect spot for a fox farm, and decided on Nuka Island. After notifying the Land Office in Juneau, they proceeded to gather materials to build a house, and Josephine readied her belongings for the move to the island.

The boat carrying Josephine to her new home was laden with crates of chickens and washtubs full of plants, plus all manner of household goods, including a huge glass-front china closet, a roll of wire screening, and anything else she had thought might come in handy in their new home and business. As they neared the island, the captain called her from her bunk to see "the most beautiful place he had ever seen."

In describing that moment, she wrote, "In an expression of mingled joy and gratitude I lifted my hands up high, took a long deep breath, and said, 'I thank God for the destiny that guided me to this place!'"

During that busy summer, with Josephine using a hammer and saw as easily as did Edward, the farm began to take shape. They built a small rectangular residence, a chicken house, and a storehouse, and installed 3,000 feet of water line to bring water to the house from a nearby creek. They were ready in September when their breeding stock of six pairs of blue foxes arrived.

Josephine and Edward settled in to a routine of preparing fox food and distributing it to feeding stations around the island. Although they caught only fleeting glimpses of the foxes in the beginning, the food regularly disappeared from the stations and it soon became apparent that the animals were thriving.

Josephine and Edward enjoyed their time on the island. They cared for the foxes and chickens all week, but took Sundays for recreation and rest. Then they rowed around the island or climbed the mountains on it, taking pleasure in discovering the varied plants and animals that shared their home.

But the couple had only three short years of their happy island life together. Edward had been in poor health for some time and Josephine had hoped that the fresh air and outdoor work would improve him. At first he did well, but then he began to fail.

His diary entry for July 24, 1923, read:

Clear and very warm weather since the 15th. This will be my last recording for a long time. Am too sick to write. Going to hospital in Seward on *Rolfh,* expected from westward today. Wife has been seining some humpies. Foxes carrying off everything in sight. Must send back help from Seward. First time in three years things have gone wrong. Hoping for the best. Finis.

Edward died of stomach cancer in Seward on August 26. Josephine, waiting for Captain Pete Sather to come on his boat, *Rolfh,* and take her to the hospital, did not arrive until August 30.

Josephine struggled to keep the fox farm business afloat for the next several months. She had enormous bills, even after gratefully accepting Pete Sather's loan of $800 to pay Edward's hospital and funeral expenses. Her son had come from Cordova when Edward was ill, but was working as a machinist there and returned to his job.

Josephine was determined to stay on Nuka Island.

"Consequently there was only one thing for me to do—marry a man who took the same delight in Nature that I did, and who would be capable and willing to take care of the fur business," she wrote.

This man would have to be someone she respected, someone who knew about engines and boats, and someone who understood the sea. So she thought of Pete Sather. She first offered him a partnership, but thought it might cause a scandal if the two of them lived on the island together. So on May 5, 1924, they entered into a marriage of convenience that served them well for thirty-seven years, although Pete was fifteen years her junior.

"People get married for business reasons only. That love talk is only foolishness anyway," Pete told her.

Government records showed Pete Sather as the fox farm operator, but Josephine remained the actual possessor of the fox farm lease. One of the first things Pete did was to build a dock, so that supplies no longer had to be rowed in from the boats by skiff. They brought lumber ashore for more building. Together, they added several rooms to the house and built a cookhouse for the fox feed, cement tanks for salting fish, a breeder shed, and a machine shop. Then they built thirty-two feed and trapping houses all around the island.

A trapping house was 6 feet by 8 feet, with a trap tunnel running across the front. The trapping season was in December, so for two months prior the foxes had to go through the tunnel to get to their food. Feeding the foxes was a never-ending job. Their staple diet was pink salmon, which Pete could easily purse-seine from his boat, by circling a school of fish and dropping the seine net around them. The fish would be salted down and stored in the large cement tanks until needed for winter food. The foxes also ate seals and sea lion meat—which, in the summer, had to be cooked—and whale meat when it was available. Josephine prepared a special digestive for the foxes made from seal fat fried with hide, hair, and chicken feathers. When meat was scarce, the foxes were fed grains mixed with seal oil and surplus eggs from the chickens. Each year they would purchase three tons of mixed rolled wheat and oats for fox feed and one ton of chicken feed from Seattle. Josephine also cooked hot cakes in seal oil, or bread soaked in seal oil, or bacon rind—all of which the foxes considered special treats.

Josephine loved taking food to the foxes, as it gave her the chance to observe them closely. She loaded up the skiff and rowed around the island, parceling out the food at various feeding stations. One year, there was a pair with eight pups at one station and the mother fox would sit on the beach waiting for her. Josephine would tease her a little, by idling the skiff just before she reached the beach, pretending that all she had for them was a bucket of fish, which they would eat only if there were nothing else left.

"Then when I'd take out the bucket of hot cakes, she'd make a grab for them. She'd never take a reasonable helping, but all she could get into her mouth. She'd carry these up to the (feeding) house, lay them on the ground, and give a series of low grunts to call the little ones."

As their routines developed and became easier to manage, Josephine had time for "what I had wished to do from the first—study the wildlife around me." She observed the blue foxes extensively, of course, as she dealt with them every day. She never ceased to be amazed at their intelligence, sense of family, resourcefulness, and the order of their homes. She studied the little squirrel families, watched the songbirds and hummingbirds that were attracted to her garden, delighted in the antics of land otters and even watched jellyfish feed.

Out of necessity Josephine used radical measures to protect her precious blue foxes from island predators. Eagles had been a problem from the very beginning. She was upset when they preyed on eggs in nests and took young foxes. Even though she was forbidden, under the terms of the fox farm lease, to kill game animals or birds, she believed "these predatory eagles were a menace to our fox-raising enterprise." She resolved to go eagle hunting and some years later stated, "I am sure that I, myself, have shot a couple of hundred, and we are still after them."

And then there were the bears. After several years, bears began appearing on the island, probably swimming over from the mainland. They robbed the feed houses at night and slept during the day, so they were difficult to locate and shoot. Josephine decided to snare the bears. This way she succeeded in killing several of them. When someone told her it was illegal to snare bears, she wrote to the game commissioner, outlining her problem, and asked him, incidentally, what wire she should use in the snares. He replied that she had violated the law, but ended his letter with, "Only No. 9 wire will hold them but remember this isn't giving you permission to snare bears." Over the years she killed seventeen of the furry raiders.

Josephine was not immune to Alaska's gold fever. In 1928, there were several gold mines around Nuka Bay. Pete hauled freight, mail, and passengers about the bay and often took Josephine with him to visit the miners. One old miner who had a good show of gold let her pan some one day. That sparked her enthusiasm for prospecting, so Pete brought her the tools from Seward and she set out for the creeks. Although she eventually found a good ledge and took out a bit of gold, Josephine decided that she preferred the more reliable career of fox farming to the back-breaking work of mining.

During the forty years that Josephine lived on Nuka Island, she went to Seward only every six or seven years and traveled Outside to visit friends just a couple of times. Her son, Frank, served in the Alaska Territorial House of Representatives from 1949 to 1951, and she visited him once in Fairbanks, where he lived with his wife and stepchildren. But she was content on Nuka Island and wrote, "Here in our cozy home I'll be perfectly happy to live the rest of my days. We have comfort and convenience, plenty of work to keep us busy, and an infinite variety of things to give life zest."

Nevertheless, Josephine was not lonely, as the Sather home was always open and a welcome stopping place for fishermen, prospectors, and boaters. During the war, young servicemen found in her hospitality a "home away from home."

"There's always a warm stove, always plenty of good reading matter, always a cup of hot coffee," Josephine said.

She filled her time with infinite projects, not the least of which was teaching herself English, using a dictionary as textbook. Her excellent command of the written language was evident in a four-chapter story published in *Alaska Sportsman* in 1946 about her life on Nuka Island.

Over the years the price for fox pelts declined steadily, so that by the early 1950s it was no longer profitable. Pete continued his freight, mail, and passenger service around Nuka Bay and Seward, and expanded his commercial fishing business.

In July of 1961 Pete Sather's boat was lost in a storm at sea between Nuka Bay and Seward, and he was never seen again. Josephine's son, Frank, had died in 1959. Finding herself alone, Josephine returned to her hometown of Ellmau, Austria, to live with her niece. She died there on October 13, 1964.

When Josephine left Seward, she left behind a manuscript that was a romantic and nostalgic look at her youth in pre-war Austria. It tells of a young girl, "Pauline," falling in love with a handsome but poor lad who is killed in a horse-jumping accident. Devastated, she thinks she will never love again, but is wooed by a wealthy, handsome "playboy type," who eventually wins her hand and showers her with riches. They wed and travel to America, to Massachusetts, then to Alaska. It is a charming, captivating, and detailed story that sheds some light on her early life, as it is clearly autobiographical.

Although her husband, Pete, was a tremendous help with the business, it was primarily Josephine who operated the fox farm. She skinned the foxes and performed the intricate task of preparing the pelts for market. All of these skills she taught herself by reading manuals and experimenting, while also teaching herself to read English. The articles that she wrote about her experiences gave a clear picture of a remarkable life spent in an unusual environment.

CRYSTAL BRILLIANT SNOW JENNE

1884–1968

Political Nightingale

AN ATTRACTIVE, STATELY MATRON gazed out the window of her Juneau home, looking across Gastineau Channel to Douglas Island. The setting sun cast a rosy glow against the snow-capped mountains that encircled the capital city, reflecting the icy peaks in the water below. But the woman wasn't thinking about the city that was spread out before her—the city of bustling vehicles, paved streets, the capitol, and the governor's house.

In her mind's eye, the woman saw an earlier Juneau on an April day in 1887. A forest of evergreens surrounded the few shacks set in a scant three-block area by the beach. It was raining as a young mother and father, with their three-year-old daughter and five-year-old son, made their way down the plank from the old side-wheel steamer, *Olympian,* which had just arrived from Seattle. With their luggage piled on a handcart, the Snow family walked the short distance to the Read Hotel. A family of performers, the Snows had arrived to provide classical entertainment for the miners. They had a contract for six weeks, but the little daughter ended up staying in Alaska for more than six decades.

Now it was another April, in 1934. The citizens of Alaska were preparing to elect the new members of their Territorial Legislature, and Crystal Snow Jenne was the first woman in Alaska to have her name on the ballot as a candidate for the Territorial House of Representatives. She had filed to run on the Democratic ticket, with the slogan: "Whet your axes: Down with taxes!" Little Crystal Brilliant Snow had come a long way since that rainy April day so many years ago.

Crystal Brilliant Snow was born in Sonora, California, on May 30, 1884. Her parents, George and Anna Snow, were talented performers who traveled through the gold-mining camps, entertaining the miners. When Crystal was three years old and her brother, Montgomery, was five, George was offered the chance to take a small troupe to Juneau, as an experiment in bringing classical theatre to the miners in Alaska.

A small theatre had been built in Juneau for the troupe to use. At the end of the six weeks for which they were initially booked, they were asked to stay for an additional six months to produce more plays. Legitimate theatre, as it turned out, was a resounding success in Juneau.

Even though entertaining the miners was more lucrative than joining them at their trade, George Snow was struck with "gold fever" and traveled into the Yukon to try his luck. Anna was left to eke out a living by sewing. She went into the dressmaking business and opened a dress shop, "Ladies Bazaar," with the wife of the Presbyterian minister. The second time George made the trip to the gold fields, he ended up staying away all winter. When he planned a third trip, Anna put down her foot and said, "If you go, we're going!" Anna was willing to risk the hard and bitter winter of the interior country rather than spend more time in Juneau without her husband.

In 1894, against the advice of her friends, Anna left with her husband and two young children. They took a little tugboat, the *Rustler*, up the Lynn Canal to the tiny trading post known as Dyea, and set out from there for the not-yet-infamous Chilkoot Pass. It would be another few years before Skagway was established as the "Gateway to the Gold Rush." There was no actual trail at that time, so George and his partners made one as they went. The men carried on their backs supplies to last them a whole year, taking several trips to relay them up the pass. One of their "supplies" carried up and over the pass was a three-octave organ!

While taking the last load of supplies, the party was near the top when a sudden blizzard enveloped them. They dug a deep, wide hole in the snow and covered it with the tent canvas, using as a tent pole a hastily cut sapling that George fetched from below the snow line. The other men retrieved the grub box and the Yukon stove from the sled, and when everything and everyone was inside the hole, the men banked snow against the opening for warmth. For three days and nights, the blizzard roared. On the fourth morning, a rescue party found them by sighting a little curl of smoke exiting their snow cave. Crystal and her brother had passed the time playing "igloo" with their mother and having a fine time. Only the adults realized that if the blizzard had continued another day, it would have meant disaster.

Finally making it over the pass and past Lake Laberge, the Snows followed the Yukon River to Forty-Mile, just inside the Yukon Territory near the Alaska border. There they spent the winter of 1894, while George searched for gold. Crystal and her brother were probably the only non-native children in the village. Crystal went to school for the first time there when she was ten years old, attending a mission school, where she learned to sing, pray, and say "gold" in the native language. She later said of that experience, "I can hardly remember learning much besides knitting."

CRYSTAL BRILLIANT SNOW JENNE

The following year the family traveled to Circle City and again decided to "mine for gold" with their acting skills. George and his partners built a two-story opera house, the first in Alaska, with wings on each side and a sign in front that read SNOW'S OPERA HOUSE. By this time Crystal and Monte were also performing with their parents. The children were very popular and the miners often threw money onto the stage for them. Telling about this during a 1951 radio interview in Juneau, Crystal recalled:

> My brother and I have had silver dollars and five-dollar gold pieces that they used to have in those days, with an occasional twenty-dollar gold piece, showered on the stage from the balcony in the old Opera houses, until we have had to take refuge behind the old-fashioned wings. After the downpour, we'd bow, pick up the coins, and run to each other shouting, "I could do this all night!"

When the Klondike gold rush was in full swing in 1898, the Snows moved to Dawson and George finally struck it rich. Taking the money, the family went to Seattle, where George, with grandiose ideas and poor business skills, lost everything when he invested in a large drama company. The Snows then returned to Juneau, which by that time seemed like home.

Crystal had not attended any established school while her family traveled, but had been tutored by her mother. In Juneau she was admitted to the fifth grade when she was sixteen years old. She described her schooling this way: "You can imagine my trials and tribulations, under those circumstances. At the same time I was taking a four-year Latin course and a two-year science course, I was also winding up my fifth, sixth, seventh, and eighth grade learning."

"I was valedictorian of my class at the age of twenty-one," she added, slyly.

Of course she was the valedictorian. She was the only person in the graduating class of 1905, which was only the second high-school class to graduate anywhere in Alaska.

After working as a sales clerk to earn her steamship passage, Crystal left Juneau to continue her education at the University of California in Berkeley. She studied music, hoping to become a concert vocalist, but she also earned a teaching certificate and followed that profession upon graduation. Her first teaching position was in Paso Robles, California; she then returned to Alaska to teach in the town of Douglas for the 1907–1908 school term.

The following summer Crystal went on tour, singing for miners all over Alaska. She sang in Skagway, Haines, Dawson, Fairbanks, Nome, and many of the creekside mining camps surrounding the towns. The tour inspired her to pursue her dream of studying music on the East Coast, but this vision was thwarted when she developed a serious strain on her vocal chords. The condition required surgery and caused the loss of her voice, to the extent that she could barely speak above a whisper for nearly a year.

Nevertheless, Crystal continued her plan to study in the East by merely changing her direction. She graduated from a prestigious business college, the Spencerian Commercial School in Cleveland, Ohio, where she learned business skills and earned a shorthand diploma.

In the fall of 1909, George and Anna Snow were living in Skagway, so Crystal took a job teaching there for a year. Then her parents, in poor health, moved to Seattle. Crystal found herself working at many different jobs in order to help support them. She did newspaper work, both writing articles and as secretary to the editor, and worked in Vancouver for the Yukon and Southeast Alaska Publicity Bureau. Finally she returned to teaching, taking a job in Sitka, where she also worked as secretary for the U.S. Experimental Agricultural Station. For a year she taught in the Mendenhall Valley, and then, in 1914, returned to Juneau, where she taught for two years in the school from which she had graduated.

Those nine years of varied experiences undoubtedly contributed to Crystal's belief that women deserved a more visible and influential role in society. Alaska had just received Territorial status, and the first act of the Territorial Legislature was to give women the right to vote. Crystal exercised that right at every opportunity.

In 1916, she married Charles Percival Jenne, a Juneau dentist, and the couple had three children. Corrinne was born in 1917, Charles in 1919, and Phyllis in 1921.

Even while raising her family, Crystal was very active in the life of the Juneau musical community. Having recovered her beautiful singing voice, she performed her mother's composition, *Alaska and the USA,* for President Warren G. Harding and his wife when they visited Juneau in July of 1923. She taught music for several years and often gave concerts to raise money for local charities. She directed the choirs at both the Catholic Church and the Episcopal Church for ten years.

It was not the first time she had been involved with Juneau church choirs. When she was a small child living in Juneau and attending the old log cabin Presbyterian Church, she recalled, "I sat in the choir at an age when I was so tiny I had to be lifted into the choir chairs!"

In 1934, when her youngest child, Phyllis, was thirteen years old, Crystal "threw her hat in the ring," and became the first woman to run for the Territorial House of Representatives. Although she was defeated, her political aspirations were not squelched, and she filed again for the next election.

In a 1936 letter addressed "To the Voters of Southeastern Alaska," she wrote:

I firmly believe that what is needed in our Legislature today is a real representative of the people whose qualifications are honesty, common sense, knowledge of conditions, aggressiveness, independence, and fearlessness, together with business ability and experience.

Crystal wrote all of her speeches in longhand, using notes that she jotted down on any little scrap of paper at hand. When somewhat finalized, she typed the speech, correcting and editing as she went along. Several of her speeches were written on the backs of papers that her high-school-aged children had used for their typing exercise assignments.

Although still unsuccessful in her political attempts, Crystal was undeterred. She filed to run again in 1938 and had the backing of many in the Democratic Party. This time she addressed the public:

I am proud of being one who is open to advice from all, but who takes orders from none. I have made only one political promise in my life. That was made publicly before the primary two years ago, when I said that if the Donkey threw me off I would remount at the first opportunity.

So Crystal ran, and lost, again. Her husband, Charles, died that year, without seeing his wife finally obtain her goal. She was a successful candidate, at long last, in the election of 1940, and represented the First District of Southeast Alaska in the Fifteenth Territorial Legislature. She was re-elected for another term in 1942.

Starting on the first day of her term as the only woman in the House, Crystal jotted down notes to herself, which she titled, "Idle Thoughts of a Woman Legislator, by The Honorable Crystal Snow Jenne, member, 15th session Territorial Legislature."

Here are some notable excerpts from that paper:

Well, here I am at last. Where do I go from here? Some folks might not like this desk way up here in front of the Speaker and Clerk, but I am glad they left it for me. I won't have to speak so loudly and I can hear everything.

Wonder why everyone seems to be wearing a forced smile? And company manners. Good heavens, is it possible that these other fifteen tried and true citizens are afraid I am going to ask for favored privileges?

Women Democrats, Women's Club members, Business and Professional Women, Pioneer Women, and Women Voters, are looking to you, as never before. Don't let them down now. Hop to it!

Dear, dear, I'm the odd one again . . . I vote "No" to spending the Territory's money for nothing.

I am "invited" (with apologies) to remain away from the American Legion dinner for legislators! No offence, I'm sure. The stag oratory will have little or no bearing on legislative matters, I imagine. Far be it from me to cramp the boys' style! I feel justly proud that these men all know I shall neither weep nor faint if they notify me that my presence is unwelcome.

Watch your step, Jenne. Fight for your convictions, but don't be a wind-bag. It gets you just nowhere. With honorable colleagues facts win—with the other kind, know your opponent and trump the trick.

Crystal did well during her first term in office, even though only one of the five bills she introduced was passed. She was surprised when one of her bills, which would have established a home for destitute women, at first passed unanimously. However, the next bill that was introduced, and quickly passed, contained a "rider" that made her bill invalid. That was her introduction to legislative "trickery," and she was much more careful the next time around.

When a bill by another legislator was reconsidered and passed by the House, its author publicly credited her clear oratory for its success. Because of her work in the legislature, she received favorable correspondence from Anthony Dimond, Alaska's delegate to Congress in Washington, D.C.

Her final note to herself, at the end of the session, read: "I have done my bit for Democracy and in the doing, have I not gained a proportion of strength which may some day fill a greater need? Who knows?"

When her term in the House of Representatives was over, Crystal was nominated by the Democratic Party as the first woman to run for the Territorial Senate. Despite the honor, she chose not to accept the nomination, but instead took the position of postmaster for Juneau. She served in that capacity from 1944 until 1955, declining to be known as the "Postmistress," because, as she insisted, "the position is Postmaster!" It was while Crystal was serving as postmaster that, largely due to her efforts, home delivery was begun in Juneau, on October 16, 1952. She was often heard on the radio, explaining special mailing policies and procedures to the local residents.

Crystal was also a talented creative writer. She composed music, wrote poetry, and kept interesting journals documenting her activities as an entertainer, legislator, and business professional. In 1939, Juneau Publishing published her book of historical poetry, *The Ghosts of Old Juneau.*

From 1938 until 1944, Crystal owned and operated the Forget-Me-Not Flower Shop in Juneau, and continued to be active in civic affairs. She was a member of the Alaska Federation of Women's Clubs, the Democratic Women's Club, the Juneau Women's Club, and the National Business and Professional Women's Club, serving as president of the Juneau branch of the latter.

Both of Crystal's parents were proud of their time as pioneers. George founded the Yukon Order of Pioneers as early as 1894, when the family lived in Forty-Mile, and Anna organized the Ladies of the Golden North in Seattle in 1919. Crystal too, honored her heritage and served as president of the Pioneers of Alaska, Igloo No. 6 Auxiliary, in Juneau. The first Pioneers Home, for the elderly, was created in Sitka in 1915, but it was just for men. In 1950 a new facility was built for women, and it was there that Crystal lived her last few years. She died there on June 5, 1968, and is buried in the Evergreen Cemetery in Juneau. All three of her children married and raised families in Alaska.

Throughout Crystal Snow Jenne's adult life, she maintained an interest in serving her community and promoting women as instruments of change. She often spoke to both the local and national organizations of the Business and Professional Women's Club, emphasizing the important part played by women in the political arena. She kept up with local and territorial issues, and, even at the age of seventy-two, tried an unsuccessful run for the 1956 Territorial Senate.

JESSIE SPIRO BLOOM

1887–1980

Founder of Fairbanks Girl Scouts

JESSIE SAT QUIETLY ROCKING AND nursing her baby daughter, enjoying the rest that this moment provided. Suddenly Bob burst in through the door, holding his hat in front of him. Thrusting it before her, he exclaimed, "Look, Jessie, fresh cherries!"

Although slightly annoyed at being disturbed, she looked up, smiled and wondered, "What kind of a place am I in, where a mature person could go into ecstasies over some fresh cherries?"

It had been barely a year since Jessie Spiro had married Robert Bloom in Dublin, Ireland, on May 17, 1912, and set sail on the *Mauritania* for America. They had traveled for two months by ship and rail, finally arriving in Fairbanks by steamer up the Tanana from Whitehorse. Jessie had only endured one winter in the interior of Alaska, so had not yet become accustomed to what she later called, "the vagaries of food shortages."

Jessie Spiro was born in Dublin on December 21, 1887, into a middle-class Jewish family. She, her sister, and her two brothers were encouraged to think for themselves and were recognized in the family as individuals. Literacy and good works were an integral part of the family's lifestyle. Each child, at age twelve, was allowed to obtain a public library card. With their mother as overseer, they read her required selection of classics, and then were free to make their own selections. The children also assisted their mother in her work with the Dublin Hebrew Ladies' Charitable Society.

Although the Jewish faith was observed in Jessie's home, her schooling was in the Christian schools in Dublin. She learned to respect other religions, while upholding her Jewish traditions. With her family she took advantage of the opportunities in the city, such as museums and art galleries. She was also a member of the Girl Guides.

When Jessie finished school, she worked for the next six years for her father in his print shop. In 1909, at the age of twenty-one, she moved to London, where she took a secretarial course and began working at a firm that promoted mercury vapor lights. She soon learned that women working at the firm were paid only half of what men were paid, and her dismay at this unfair practice led her to join the Women's Freedom League (WFL), where she became a dedicated suffragette.

It was while Jessie was working in London that Robert Bloom visited there in December 1910. Bob was born in Lithuania in 1878, but had lived in Dublin from an early age. When he was nineteen, he had traveled to Seattle, and then joined the gold-seekers walking over Chilkoot Pass. Disenchanted with mining, he moved on to Fairbanks and opened a general store, ultimately becoming a successful retail businessman. He had come to London to help settle the estate of one of his brothers when he became reacquainted with his second cousin, Jessie. After a short courtship in London, they each returned to visit their respective families in Dublin, and Bob proposed marriage. It was decided that Bob would go back to Alaska, and then return the following year to wed Jessie.

In 1912, Jessie and Bob were married in a private Jewish ceremony in Dublin, and then set sail for America. One of their daughters later wrote, "Mother was equipped with the usual bride's

A CROPPED PHOTO OF JESSIE SPIRO BLOOM, 1912

trousseau of those days for one setting out to start a life in the 'Colonies,' trunks with linen, cutlery, and a dinner service. I recall her showing the last plate of that service to a friend many years later and it coming apart in her hands."

Bob was quite well respected in the Fairbanks community and Jessie felt very welcome. On her first full day in town, she received three separate invitations, one to join the Presbyterian Ladies' Aid Society, one to go walking, and one to meet other women at tea.

Shortly after Jessie and Bob arrived in Alaska, the federal government granted Home Rule to the territory, giving Alaskans the privilege of governing themselves. The newly formed legislature met the next year, 1913, in Juneau, and its first act was to grant voting privileges to women. Jessie recalled, "I was thrilled when I heard about it . . . that I had come to a country full of opportunity, and had changed from a Subject of King George, to a full-fledged citizen of a flourishing democracy." Bob commented at the time, "Leave it to the Pioneers of Alaska, they know how to appreciate their women."

The Blooms' first daughter, Meta, was born on April 5, 1913, and the event was noted on the front page of the *Fairbanks Daily News-Miner*. Such was life in a small town.

In February of 1914, the women of Fairbanks came together in a meeting at the courthouse to acquaint themselves with both the election process and the issues. According to Jessie, there were about one hundred women in attendance. She wrote about that gathering:

> We in England were fighting for the Vote and so had acquainted ourselves with the various issues involved, and when we should get it, we hoped we would be able to use it to advantage, but in Alaska where there had been no campaign, it had been thrust upon us, it was a different matter, we might abuse our great gifts, through ignorance.

Several women spoke about suffrage in other states, notably Wyoming, Oregon, and Colorado. It was mentioned that the women in Colorado had formed civic clubs to study various problems. So Jessie "rose and put a motion to the floor," suggesting the formation of a similar club. After carrying the motion unanimously, the women "adjourned to arrange about drawing up some rules for the Fairbanks Women's Civic Club."

Soon Jessie became pregnant again, and Bob insisted that she take Meta and return to Dublin for the second baby's birth. In July, as war broke out in Europe, Jessie and Meta left Alaska. Deborah Bloom was born in Dublin on December 6, 1914. The two years that Jessie and her babies spent in Ireland were unsettled times there. Not only was there fighting in Europe and Britain, but also rebellion in Ireland. Jessie was relieved to sail for home in June of 1916, and was thrilled to finally arrive on Alaskan soil in August.

Bob had not been idle during his family's time away. The little, two-room frame house where Jessie had first set up housekeeping had undergone some welcome renovations. It now had a well and pump, a bathroom, and a kitchen sink, complete with hot and cold running water.

Autumn was always a busy time for Jessie, or for anyone keeping house in Fairbanks in the early years. First, the year's order of staples would arrive on the last riverboat that came in before freeze-up, so storage had to be found for the cans of tomatoes, peas, corn, fruit, and, of course, the "Alaska cow" (evaporated milk), as well as for dried fruits, beans, peas, and cereals. Some of the Blooms' supplies were kept in Bob's store warehouse. The garden was ready for harvest, so the carrots, turnips, potatoes, beets, and celery were stored in the root cellar underneath the kitchen. The cabbage was made into sauerkraut, put up in glass jars, and added to the root cellar. Berries were also ripe then, so Jessie was busy making jellies and jam.

As the days and nights grew colder, the back porch became cold storage and kept meats and baked goods frozen. One year Jessie had too many carrots to store in the root cellar. She found a recipe for carrot pudding, made them all into pudding, and froze them on the porch. "That winter," she wrote, "my desert [sic] problem was solved, all I had to do was break off a chunk of carrot pudding, put it in the double boiler early in the morning, and leave it on the cook stove, and let it thaw out gradually and then steam until ready to be eaten."

In May of 1917, their third daughter, Olga, was born, and the following summer she gave birth to Ruth. That fall Jessie felt that Meta, at five, should start her formal education, but she was too young for the Fairbanks public school. Undaunted, she began the first Fairbanks kindergarten class in her home. A primary school teacher, Florence Smith Kelley, assisted her in planning the curriculum. The class of six children met for two hours in the afternoon. Giving credence to the program, Jessie obtained certification as a kindergarten teacher in 1921, with a correspondence course from the Bureau of Education in Washington, D.C.

With these additional activities Jessie still found time to adhere to a schedule of a daily walk, which she believed to be of utmost importance to good health, and which she continued to do, as possible, for her whole life. She insisted, "Even at fifty below, I manage to get outdoors, for five or ten minutes at a time. Some people will say, 'Is it worth the effort to bundle up to go out for ten minutes?' I always answer that it is, definitely."

In 1922, the Alaska Agricultural College opened its doors on a hill 4 miles outside of Fairbanks. Bob was a member of the Board of Regents at that time, so he was very busy Jessie said, helping it "get into shape to open its portals to its aspiring scholars." She described the event:

The opening ceremony took place on a bright September Morning in 1922. The children from the Public School, about two hundred, were all lined up on either side of the Hill, where the College was built, and the members of the Faculty and the Board of Regents, and the Governor passed through the Body Guard that they formed, and the opening ceremony was performed by the Governor, in a very simple speech . . . I had the wonderful feeling of helping to build something more than a mere Agricultural College and School of Mines, I had the feeling of helping to bring into the Pioneer Community, some of the background of learning and culture that was the inheritance of so many of us that lived and worked for the Territory.

On July 15, 1923, President Warren G. Harding drove in the Golden Spike to signify the completion of the Alaska Railroad from Seward to Fairbanks. By then all of Jessie's daughters were old enough for primary school, and she was eager for a break from the harsh winters of Fairbanks. Bob was unable to leave his business, but suggested that she take the girls to Seattle for the winter. How much easier and more comfortable this trip must have seemed to Jessie, as they were able to board the train in Fairbanks for Seward, and take the steamer from there to Seattle.

Jessie anticipated with pleasure the opportunity for the girls to be part of a Jewish community in Seattle. They were the only Jewish family in Fairbanks at one time, but they still kept the customs part of their home life. They lit the Shabbat candles on Friday night and read a Bible story before bedtime, so the girls knew that Friday was different from every other night of the week. Even though the Blooms could not keep a kosher kitchen, they followed basic Jewish dietary laws. The girls participated in community events held at local churches, but did not attend Sunday school or celebrate Christmas. They did, however, exchange presents with their friends.

Jessie and her daughters settled very happily into a Jewish neighborhood in Seattle, where the girls were able to participate in synagogue activities. Jessie enjoyed being in the area itself, as it reminded her of Dublin. She enjoyed being able to keep a kosher kitchen and follow all of the traditions. In fact, she enjoyed it so much that she and her girls stayed for two years.

When they arrived back in Fairbanks in 1925, the family found a surprise—Bob had built them a new house. Although Jessie was not happy at first, she had to admit that the house was beautiful. It was two stories, with beveled windowpanes and a spiral staircase that Bob had salvaged from another house, and a hardwood floor, which had come from a dance hall that he bought and demolished.

That fall, Jessie, remembering her experiences as a Girl Guide in Dublin, organized the first Girl Scout troop in Alaska. The initial members were seven girls from a sewing club at the Presbyterian Church, where the troop continued to meet for the first year. In the summer the girls wanted to go camping, so they put on a talent show at the Legion Hall in June, raising enough money to pay for transportation and supplies for twenty campers. They bought a tent, rented a cabin at Birch Lake, and were off for their grand adventure. The experience was so successful that it was repeated the next year.

In order to register their camp with the national Girl Scout Headquarters, Jessie filled out the appropriate forms, noting for one question that they had used canned milk. She also wrote about a spectacular display of Northern Lights experienced by the campers. When Headquarters reported that they would mention the camp in their national bulletin, the leaders and girls could hardly wait for the bulletin to arrive. Imagine their surprise when the most impressive note regarding their camp was not the Northern Lights, but the use of canned milk!

Before Jessie and her daughters had gone to Seattle, they had become interested in studying the many types of mushrooms that grew across the river near Graehl. They had used an article in a 1923 issue of *National Geographic* to help with identification. The residents in Graehl often referred to "Jessie's mushroom project." She continued her "project" with the scouts, and today a pamphlet of the Farthest North Girl Scout Council includes a photograph of girls identifying mushrooms with Jessie Bloom at Harding Lake. Jessie remained the Girl Scout leader for the next three years.

In 1928, when her oldest daughter was fifteen and her youngest was ten, Jessie felt compelled to provide a more traditional education for them. Bob remained in Fairbanks, while Jessie and the girls spent the remainder of their teenage years in Dublin. It was nine years later in 1937 when Jessie returned to Bob and their home in Alaska. Their daughters, following their parents' direction and inspiration, became professionals and respected members in their own communities. Two became medical doctors, one became an architect, and one a linguist.

Although Jessie was happy to return to her husband, she did not relish the prospect of more Alaska winters. She hoped that Bob would retire so they could move to Seattle, but he was not ready to close his business, and was still very much involved in community affairs.

At the outbreak of World War II, military personnel expanded their presence in Fairbanks. The Jewish Welfare Board asked Bob to be a lay rabbi for the Alaskan interior, and he and Jessie became unofficial chaplains for the Jewish servicemen stationed there. In the November 24, 1958, issue of *Congress Weekly*, Philip S. Bernstein of Rochester, New York, wrote in a letter to the editor:

> Suddenly vast numbers of GIs descended on Alaska and the Aleutians. Fairbanks was headquarters for the Air Command. Hundreds, probably thousands, of Jews were among them. The Blooms became their parents, their friends, their counselors, their chaplains, until, and even after, the Jewish chaplains arrived.

Innumerable Jewish GIs turned to them for friendship, for a loan, for Jewish cooking. When I was in Alaska for Passover in 1943, I found that Jessie Bloom was herself chopping up what seemed tons of gefilte fish for the military *sedorim*. . . . This Jewish ex-sourdough and his Dublin bride have an honored place in the history of the frozen North.

In 1950, Bob finally agreed to retire, and the Blooms moved Outside and bought a house in Seattle on Puget Sound. Robert Bloom died in Seattle in April of 1974, at the age of ninety-five. Jessie continued to maintain close ties with her Fairbanks friends and the growing Jewish community there until her death in December of 1980 at the age of ninety-two.

Following the end of the war, Jessie began writing down her memories and impressions of living in Alaska. Her reminiscences provide invaluable glimpses into the life of a Fairbanks pioneer: amusing descriptions of how to dress to go outdoors in extremely cold weather; planning two weeks worth of meals from the back porch "freezer"; seeing a neighbor who didn't like the looks of the meat at the butcher shop take her gun, walk about a quarter of a mile from Fairbanks, and shoot three ptarmigan; and fetching ice from the river in winter and melting it to get water soft enough for washing delicate materials. Her written memories provide a wealth of information about the early days of Fairbanks.

Jessie is remembered and honored by the Farthest North Girl Scout Council in Fairbanks as their founder. The now-permanent camp at Birch Lake is today called "Camp Jessie Bloom."

CLARA HICKMAN RUST

1890-1978

The Mother of Fairbanks

IT WASN'T EXACTLY THE KIND OF WEDDING A GIRL envisions in her dreams. First, the miner groom barely made it into town in time for the 7:00 P.M. ceremony because he hadn't received the letter confirming the date. He had found out by accident when a neighbor told him, just that morning, that the wedding announcement was in the paper!

Second, he had sent the bride some money via a friend, and the "friend" had lost it in a poker game. At the last minute, the groom had had to sell one of his sled dogs to pay for the wedding expenses.

Finally married, Clara and Jess Rust traveled from Fairbanks to the mine on Little Eldorado Creek, where they would share a small cabin with Jess's two partners. They rode in a heavily loaded sled, which was topped with Clara's mattress and pulled by an old nag who sat down every few miles. Exhausted, Clara looked forward to the little curtained-off sleeping area and the comfortable wolf robe covering the bed.

After a hot supper, but before she had a chance to relax, there was a commotion from outside. A dozen or more miners surrounded the cabin, swinging lanterns, banging on pans, and ringing sleigh bells. Swarming into the tiny room, they brought cakes, loaves of sourdough bread, wine, and whiskey. They greeted Clara with a hug and pounded Jess on the back. What a shivaree—there hadn't been a bride on the Eldorado for a long time, and the miners were intent on providing Clara with a memorable welcome party. Some of the men had dressed up like women, so Clara wouldn't feel "lonesome." Clara laughed until her sides ached.

It was a good thing Clara could laugh. She would often find that a sense of humor was a necessity for life in the frontier town of Fairbanks.

Clara Hickman was born in Seattle in 1890, joining her brother, Thayne, who was two years old. Clara's little sister, Beth, was born in 1896.

Zach Hickman struggled to support his children and his wife, Martha. The year before Clara's birth, her father's printing shop was destroyed in the great Seattle fire. As successive business ventures failed, life became more difficult for the family. Clara was obliged to quit school in the eighth grade and took her first job, dipping chocolates in a candy factory. After two unsuccessful attempts at starting businesses in Alaska, Zach tried again in 1907, taking his wife and Beth with him to Fairbanks where Thayne had found work on the river barges.

Clara stayed behind in Seattle, on her own at the age of sixteen. But the following year, Thayne drowned in the Chatanika River, and she left for Fairbanks to comfort her grieving mother.

It was late summer when Clara left Seattle on the steamship *Northwestern* for the journey to St. Michael, on the western coast of Alaska. There she transferred to a smaller river steamboat, the *Susie,* which would take her up the Yukon to an even smaller boat for the rest of the trip up the Tanana River to Chena. She made the last few miles to Fairbanks in a rowboat. The entire trip took thirty-two

CLARA RUST STANDING IN FRONT OF A MINE AT LITTLE ELDORADO

days. While traveling to Alaska, Clara began writing in a journal and continued to do so throughout her life.

In Fairbanks the family lived in a small three-room log cabin on Eighth Street. A lean-to in back served as the kitchen, and in her parents' bedroom, there was a bed that folded against the wall to provide more space during the day. The walls were covered with burgundy burlap. On top of the wood plank floors was a layer of newspapers for insulation and over that was canvas, which had been tacked down at the edges and painted green. Precious water, which came from a neighbor's well, was kept in two five-gallon cans with wooden lids. The little outhouse was down a short path and had a piece of caribou fur tacked to the toilet seat.

Although the small town of Fairbanks was a far cry from the big city where Clara had lived, it was a thriving community, and seemed more substantial than the little gold rush camps that came and went so quickly. By the time Clara arrived in the fall of 1908, Fairbanks was barely six years old. There were 8,000 inhabitants, not only miners and businessmen, but also their wives and children. Clara's father now owned *The Daily News,* one of three newspapers in Fairbanks, and there were four of those newfangled machines—automobiles—around town. There were schools, churches, banks, and many retail shops comfortably stocked with enough items to provide the population all their needs until freight could arrive again from Outside in the spring.

The women had formed social clubs, and the men had banded together in lodge organizations. As little mining could be done in the winter, it was a very busy "in town" time. There were dances, church meetings, study clubs, and theatrical performances. In fact, the very first night Clara spent in Fairbanks, she accompanied her mother to theatre practice and immediately found herself part of the cast.

Clara quickly found work at Mary Anderson's Dry Goods and Dress Shop, the first of many jobs she would have in Fairbanks. Always cognizant of her large size, Clara appreciated Mary's eye for fashion and her help in dressing to emphasize her hourglass figure. As an attractive young woman with a beautiful smile and friendly personality, Clara was soon stepping out to many social activities. One of her frequent escorts was a young miner, Jess Rust. When Jess escorted her to a formal ball one winter evening, the temperature was below zero and she wore under her evening gown wool tights, heavy stockings, and warm boots. Over her gown she wore a sweater, heavy coat, two scarves, and mittens.

Clara's parents still had financial difficulties, and often quarreled. In the fall of 1909, her mother returned to Seattle, taking Beth with her. Her parents divorced, and before moving to Dawson, Clara's father deeded the family's little log cabin to her. He then sold *The Daily News* to W. F. Thompson, who changed the name to *The Daily*

News-Miner. Clara had become fond of Fairbanks, and of Jess, so she chose to stay. The following year, on October 25, 1910, Clara and Jess were married and moved to the mine on the Little Eldorado.

Clara referred to herself as "the greenest bride on the creeks." Even though she had been on her own before, she had not mastered cooking. Jess showed her how to make bread, doughnuts, and delicacies. One day he left her to make applesauce from dried apples.

"Just put them in a kettle with some water, boil them to make them soft, and add sugar," he had instructed. By the time he got home, she had apples in every pan and kettle in the cabin! The story was laughed about all up and down the creek, and was just fading into memory when the same thing happened with rice. But soon Clara mastered the miner wife's life, and even found a little gold dust of her own when Jess set her up with a "rocker" box to wash gravel from the creek.

Jess's mother, Cora Madole, eventually moved in with them. She was a partner in the mining venture, having mortgaged a house in Seattle to help finance it, and was a big help with the cooking. She and Clara put in a little garden around the edges of the cookhouse, and even grew some vegetables on the roof of the barn.

But in July a bad decision by Jess's partners cost them the mine and their dreams of riches were washed away. Mother Madole took a job cooking at a café, Clara went to work cooking for neighboring miners, and Jess took a job as a telephone lineman for the rest of the summer.

In the fall Clara and Jess moved back to Fairbanks into the little log house that now belonged to Clara. Jess sawed lumber and Clara worked again for Mary Anderson, part-time, because she was expecting their first child. The little girl was born in March of 1912. A year and a half later, a second daughter came along. Clara objected when Jess bought a used washing machine to help with the diapers, but when he tried to sell it, she had "warmed up to it" and objected yet again.

Jess began working in the boiler room of the Northern Commercial Company, a large trading company that supplied the city's power, as well as groceries and other goods. This was a well-paid job that provided free lights and telephone as well as discounts at the company store. The future looked brighter. Clara was elected into the Fairbanks Pioneer Women of Alaska in 1916 as "charter member number 18," and later served twice as the organization's president.

The next few years brought a third daughter, June, to join Lila and Cora, and in 1920, Clara gave birth to a son and Jess proudly named him Jesse Worthington Rust Jr.

Over the years there were other changes as well, especially to the little log cabin. The water was still brought in, but now it came by a hand pump into a clean tub. Baths were still a "bucket by-the-stove" arrangement. A new room was added prior to the birth of the next baby, another boy, named George. At last Clara and Jess had a bedroom of their own, and the old pull-down bed was removed from what was now the dining room. There was also a brand new Lang stove in the kitchen.

But after the new baby, money was tight again, and Clara went to work at the American Hand Laundry, earning 75 cents an hour. She saved time by washing her own linens at the laundry. She continued to work at the laundry full-time for the next three years, then worked part-time for several more years.

One day, while Clara was rushing to get work done in the kitchen and give the children hot baths, little Jess was scalded when he fell into a kettle of boiling water. After waiting eight long hours for the doctor to arrive, the toddler was rushed to the hospital with severe burns. It was several days before tiny Jess was pronounced out of danger, and he carried burn scars for the rest of his life. The doctor was so apologetic for not realizing the severity of the situation from Clara's several frantic calls that he did not charge for his services.

July 16, 1923, was the hottest day in the history of Fairbanks. The temperature reached 105 degrees as Clara and the children stood among the crowd waiting to see President Warren G. Harding arrive after the Golden Spike Ceremony in Nenana. Clara watched proudly as Jess drove an open touring car carrying Herbert Hoover and other members of the party.

In the spring of 1926 Jess taught Clara to drive a borrowed automobile. Shortly thereafter, the Rusts inherited some money from a dear bachelor friend and purchased a brand new blue Dodge Star touring car, which they drove for many years.

That summer Jess was asked to go on a four-month expedition up the Yukon into Canada, as a paid guide and riverboat captain for Olaus Murie, the Rusts' young naturalist friend. Murie had often stayed with them while visiting Fairbanks, and had married their next-door neighbor, Mardy Thomas. Now the young couple, along with their nine-month-old baby, was off to the wilderness to study the mating habits of ducks and geese.

Clara encouraged Jess to go, even though she was pregnant with their sixth child. She had already made arrangements to have the baby at the hospital, rather than at home, as she had done with their other children, and Jess had received permission from his boss to take leave. Jess went on his expedition, and baby Beth was born on a hot August day, while her father was at the little village of Old Crow. He didn't receive word of her birth until he reached Fort Yukon, on his way home in September.

That winter Clara took a job at the Northern Commercial Company for the Christmas holidays. She was the first woman to work at the largest store in Fairbanks. She continued to work at the laundry to help with expenses that were ever necessary for their house.

Although raising a family and often working full-time, Clara still found time for the community. She helped to organize the first

Fairbanks Parent-Teacher Association and also helped Jessie Bloom with the first Girl Scout Troop in Alaska. She and Jess loved to dance, so she started the Sourdough Dance Club.

In 1931, Clara and Beth took the train to visit friends living near Curry, halfway between Fairbanks and Anchorage. While they were away, the Tanana and Chena Rivers overflowed. Upon their return, Jess met his wife and daughter at the train and brought with him tall rubber boots for them to wear. Even though their house was on high ground, the basement flooded, covering the furnace, water pump, and boxes of irreplaceable mementoes.

The next year, Clara changed jobs again. After many years at the laundry, Clara became one of the "Hello Girls" working the PBX switchboard, which linked Fairbanks to the little towns of Fox, Dome, Vault, Cleary, Ester, and Chatanika. She put together her own telephone book, listing the subscribers in alphabetical order and the numbers in numerical order. She attached her earphones, adjusted her mouthpiece, and connected the community for the next nine years, working ten hours a day, five days a week.

Each extra bit of money went into home improvement. After many years of planning, a second story had been added, the kitchen modernized, and there was even indoor plumbing. The little log cabin had become a house.

The first Rust family bride was Lila, who married at Christmastime in 1932. As the years passed, the other Rust children, too, married and moved out of the house. Two of the girls stayed in Fairbanks, while the other children scattered around other parts of Alaska and even ventured Outside.

In 1948, at an age when most people think about retirement, Clara and Jess homesteaded on 160 acres near Badger Road, outside of Fairbanks. They started with a tent, and then built a five-room log cabin, which eventually became a modern house.

"I peeled every single log that went into that house and garage," Clara told an interviewer several years later. She also helped clear the land and laid out a vegetable garden.

That same year she was the first Fairbanksan to be named Soroptimist "Woman of the Year," and the next year was honored as Fairbanks "Mother of the Year."

A few years after Jess died in 1956, Clara moved to Seattle, where Jess Jr. lived with his family. But she missed Fairbanks and her friends, and so in 1963, at the age of seventy-three, she packed up her automobile and drove home on the Alaska Highway.

Clara moved into the Fairbanks Pioneer Home in 1967, and began writing a newspaper column, "News of the Pioneers." The articles were published in *Jessen's Daily* until 1969, and then in the *Fairbanks Daily News-Miner*. She belonged to the Fairbanks Republican Club, and was proud to be chosen in 1972 to cast one of Alaska's three electoral votes for President.

Using her journals as reference, Clara wrote stories for *Alaska Sportsman* and *Alaska Journal* about her years as a bride on the Eldorado, her experience as a "Hello Girl," and her trip to Alaska in 1908.

Eventually, Clara convinced Jo Anne Wold to collaborate with her and write the story of her life. Jo Anne was a remarkable young woman who had contracted polio as a child and was wheelchair-bound. Using a pencil in her teeth and a typewriter, she wrote a number of articles and books about Fairbanks history.

Using Clara's twelve journals, as well as three years worth of conversations and interviews, Jo Anne produced a charming and readable book, *This Old House: The Story of Clara Rust, Alaska Pioneer,* published in 1976. Jo Anne wrote of life in Fairbanks and the Rust family, using details from Clara's journals to make the stories come to life. Clara loved the book and delighted in signing copies of it for her friends.

Clara died at the Pioneers Home in Fairbanks on March 4, 1978.

Clara Rust was not an Alaska newsmaker. She did not write any important legislation nor did she head any statewide or national organizations. She did not attend a well-known school or university. She was not a famous entertainer or author. Her actions were not legendary or unusual.

But Clara Rust was a typical, working-class Alaska pioneer. She came to a new place and faced unknown hardships. She learned to hunt and fish, and could "dress out" a moose or caribou with ease. She loved to be outside in the wilderness with her husband. She suffered loss, endured cold winters and mosquito summers, and became involved in community activities, working to make life better for herself and her family. Her story is important because it is the story of so many women who settled in Alaska in the early days and helped to make it the civilized and interesting place that it is today.

BENZIE OLA "RUSTY" DOW

1894-1989

Trucker and Artist

MOST OF THE PAGES IN THE DIARIES ARE BLANK, but there is this brief entry for June 1944: "Delivered a load of cement to Whitehorse; hauled army machinery from there to Dawson Creek; picked up another load of reconditioned tires and brought them to Fairbanks."

Thus Benzie "Rusty" Dow described her remarkable feat of driving the newly constructed Alcan Highway alone—the first woman to do so. As she said, it was "just another job."

Even today "driving the Alcan" conjures up images of long, desolate stretches of roads, made uneven from permafrost bulges; icy spots on bridges over high chasms; and unexpected problems to be faced along the road connecting Alaska to the "lower 48."

The widely available annual publication, *The Milepost,* now describes the highway in detail. It provides excellent, detailed maps, tells where along the way to find the next gas station, restaurant, museum, or rest stop, and even suggests where to look beside the road for wildlife. But today's Alcan has been much improved from that original, quickly built Army utility road that Rusty drove in 1944.

After the bombing of Pearl Harbor on December 7, 1941, it was feared that the Japanese might invade Alaska. They actually did so, and occupied Attu, the westernmost island of the Aleutians, for almost a year, beginning in June 1942, until being driven off in May of 1943.

A route was necessary to move troops and supplies overland quickly. Work on the link to Alaska through Canada began on March 9, 1942, and the final connection was made on September 25 of that year. By October it was possible, but not easy, to drive the entire highway. The road followed old Indian trails, existing winter roads, and flight paths along a chain of airfields from Edmonton, Alberta, to Fairbanks.

To be chosen for this particular trucking assignment was exciting for Rusty Dow, but she might have said that she had trained for it all of her life.

Benzie Ola Scott was born in 1894 in Wallace Station, Texas, to John and Ward Scott. She had three brothers: Homer, Zoell, and John. The family lived on a ranch when she was a child, and she had driven a truck for as long as she could remember.

"I was born in Texas and learned to handle horses. It was nothing to learn to drive a truck. It was just nature," she once explained.

For most of her childhood, the family moved around from place to place, stopping for a time when there was work to be had. Rusty recalled, "I know all about being raised on the prairie. They'd go so far and pull up a team and put up a tent. We never rented a place, just lived in the country. It wasn't uncommon. We weren't unusual."

Her father, John, was a top-grade carpenter, but when there was no carpentry work available, he would take what was offered. Often he and all the other members of the family as well, would pick cotton and do other seasonal work.

And wherever they stopped, the children would go to school. When Rusty was fifteen or sixteen, she finished high school in Carlsbad, New Mexico. It was probably there that she received her

RUSTY DOW SITTING ON THE HOOD OF THE MILITARY TRUCK
SHE DROVE ON THE ALCAN

nickname of "Rusty" because of her curly red hair. The family then moved out west to Los Angeles, California.

Rusty liked working outdoors and began trucking produce from farms to the markets, using her family's half-ton Chevy truck. When her brother, Zoell, invited the family to come up and join him in Alaska's Matanuska Valley, Rusty jumped at the chance. The Chevy was shipped up with her, first on a boat to Seward, then by train to Palmer.

When she arrived in Palmer in 1934, there were few roads and fewer motorized vehicles. Her first contract job was to load up the mail that came in on the train from Anchorage and transfer it to the Palmer Post Office. That grew into a trucking service, and Rusty began hauling freight from Palmer to and from the Independence Mine. The Independence was a lucrative gold producer, located about 17 miles north of Palmer by way of a gravel road. At one time the mine employed 204 men.

Since a lot of what she hauled for the miners was their laundry, Rusty took a lease on the only laundry business in Palmer and ran that, too. When the road into Anchorage was finally built, she bought an old, four-door Oldsmobile sedan and started a charter service back and forth. She would pick up the miners when they got off their shifts and drive them into Anchorage.

"Nothing for me to have six of them clean passed out of the picture on the return trip home, but they were all fine men, would have fought for me any time. Used to haul them into the truck and deliver them safe and sound to the bunkhouse," she recalled.

On one of those runs up to the mine, Rusty stopped at the Fishhook Inn and picked up a young miner, Russell Dow. Russ had seen Rusty before, but had never met her. In 1935 he had come to Palmer with a friend from New Hampshire who wanted to take some movies of the Matanuska colonists' site. The locals insisted that he first take some pictures at the railroad station of their Rusty unloading a boxcar. They were quite proud of her and bragged that she was stronger than any woman and most men.

Russ had returned to Alaska to stay in 1937. It was two years later that Rusty "picked him up" at the Fishhook Inn. Rusty was quite popular at the local dances, as there were lots of men around, but not many women. She also had her own car while most men did not. Russ claimed that the town's entire female population was made up of "the schoolteacher, a nurse, and Rusty."

With Rusty's cheerful manner and strong personality, she could have had her choice of men. She had many friends among them, and several may have seen themselves as possible suitors. But Rusty wasn't interested in marriage.

Nevertheless, ten months after meeting Russell Dow—who, unbeknownst to him, was twenty-one years younger than Rusty— the couple married and moved to Anchorage. Russ took a civilian construction job with the U.S. military and Rusty continued her trucking service between Palmer and Anchorage.

In 1941, Rusty received a letter from the employment service, offering her a job. She was told that the "general" had heard of a capable woman driver and asked that she be hired. She accepted and started doing civilian work for the military driving a Carryall—a panel truck with two facing benches running the length of the inside. At first she just rode around Anchorage, driving women to their jobs and carrying mail from the train station to the offices. Soon she was driving for the officers.

The following year, General Simon B. Buckner Jr. sent orders to Colonel B. B. Talley to hire a few very skillful drivers for a special assignment. The Whittier Tunnel was near completion from Whittier on Prince William Sound, to Portage on Turnagain Arm, south of Anchorage. This tunnel was of great military importance, as it would cut 52 miles off the distance from the sea to the interior of Alaska and expand the Alaska railroad system by adding a rail line from Prince William Sound. The military officers, or the "Big Brass," would be coming to Alaska for the "Holing Through" ceremony and banquet. Held on November 20, 1943, that ceremony celebrated the successful meeting in the middle of the digging from both ends of the tunnel, at Whittier and Portage.

Rusty knew she was an excellent driver and very much wanted this assignment. She rather pointedly made her wishes known to Colonel Talley and was consequently chosen to drive in the convoy carrying officers. Because the route was covered with ice and snow, Rusty took a temporary trail along the side of the mountain. There were jagged rocks rising vertically on one side and a deep chasm down to the glacier on the other. Skillfully and confidently, Rusty delivered the officers along the tunnel route. They were safe and impressed.

During this time, there were occasional air-raid alerts in Anchorage, when Japanese bombers were thought to be an imminent threat. As both Rusty and Russell worked for the military, each had an individual assignment when the alert siren sounded. Russell was to go to the base and get into a basement there, so he would be available to drive emergency construction vehicles if needed. Rusty, because she drove for the officers, was in charge of the "government car." Her orders were to take the car way out into the woods south of the city, find some little road, and hide it in the brush until the "all clear" sounded. This would keep the car safe if bombs were actually dropped on the base. Fortunately, an actual air raid never occurred.

It was General Buckner who was responsible for giving Rusty her most famous assignment. One day they met while she was unloading a truck.

Rusty told the story this way:

Got talkin', the way we do in Alaska. While the General and I were discussing things I mentioned that I'd like to do two things before I died—drive the Burma Road and the Alcan Highway. Can't do much about the first, the General said, but the second holds some possibilities.

Although driving the Alcan had been her own idea, Rusty was still surprised one day when she was called into the major's office. There she was told that on orders from General Buckner, she had two hours to report to Merrill Field in Anchorage where she would be flown to Fairbanks and given further instructions. In Fairbanks she was assigned a ten-wheel Studebaker 6x6, and told to familiarize herself with its characteristics and peculiarities. She later described this truck as being "as temperamental as a wolverine after a long winter!" Although the truck had many mechanisms that were out of order, and the tires were recapped and worn, the other drivers in the motor pool assured her that its condition was not that unusual. The men gave her good information and were helpful in answering her questions regarding road conditions and stopping points.

Although extremely confident of her own abilities, she sensed their skepticism: "This was a man's job on a man's road—built by men in its entirety, and I was thoroughly conscious that my position was that of an intruder on man's domain."

On the morning of Sunday, June 4, 1944, Rusty's truck was loaded with five tons of concrete and bound for Whitehorse, Yukon Territory. Pictures were taken for the newspapers and Corps of Engineers Transportation Officer Captain C. H. Ax bade her "Goodbye, good luck, and keep her rolling." He handed her a letter of introduction and eight packs of K-rations for emergencies.

The road just out of Fairbanks was well maintained. When she stopped at the Blue Fox, one of Alaska's oldest roadhouses, she signed her first autograph. At the next little town of Big Delta, she had her first flat tire. The repair shop was closed on Sunday, but she was able to locate some "deadline" trucks—ones that didn't run but were kept around for needed parts—and pick up a couple of spares. By the time she reached Tok Junction, where she would spend the first night, it was after dinnertime and the mess hall was being used to show movies. Once the films ended and the audience of soldiers recovered from the surprise of finding a woman truck driver standing at the back door, she was able to get a bite to eat before retiring.

She was late starting the next day because of needed truck repairs. Later, realizing that she had driven past the post marking the Alaska/Yukon border, Rusty turned around and went back to autograph it. It was well after midnight when she finally arrived at Destruction Bay Post on the edge of Kluane Lake.

After a few hours of sleep, she had breakfast with the soldiers on duty there. The date was June 6, and she listened eagerly as they told her the news that had come over the midnight radio broadcast about the successful invasion on the beaches of Normandy.

On her fourth day of travel, she contacted the Whitehorse command post by phone and got orders on where to unload the cement. Her "beaten-up old truck," as she referred to it, had to be replaced, but there was one available that was the same model, so she had no problem driving it. The truck was loaded with tractor parts and baggage, more interviews were given and photographs taken, and Rusty was on her way again.

Over the course of the next three days, Rusty drove through billowing clouds of smoke from two forest fires that left sparks still blowing across the road. She endured dizzying curves along the blasted-out cliffs shouldering Muncho Lake, and she lost time repairing a broken wire when the motor quit.

On her seventh day on the road, Rusty got another late start and was too late for dinner by the time she got to Blueberry Station. She broke out one of the K-rations, only to discover it had been contaminated by gasoline. So she decided to press on to Fort St. John. Unfortunately, the fort was not visible from the road. Finally, about 2:30 in the morning, she came to a station.

It was Dawson Creek! She had driven the Alcan in seven days.

Her successful arrival was met with admiration from the military and much interest from the residents of Dawson Creek. There were the usual photographs and interviews, plus some genuinely appreciated meals.

By the next day Rusty's cargo had been unloaded and replaced with a load of tires for Fairbanks. The trip back was relatively uneventful, and a day or so shorter, as the stops were familiar to her and she was expected all along the way.

The day that Rusty finished her remarkable assignment was her fiftieth birthday. This, however, was not noted, as Rusty *never* mentioned or divulged her age.

Rusty continued to drive for the military until the end of the war. Then she and Russell took a few months off and drove Outside, to see if there were any other places they would like to live. They traveled down to Denver, east to New Hampshire, around the coast to New Orleans, and, finally, back up north. Alaska, they had decided, would always be home.

They found a little piece of land on the Knik River, near Palmer, and homesteaded. There they built their own log cabin, with Rusty doing much of the hauling and placing of logs.

"Handling 20-foot logs is like lifting pencils if you have the right tools and know-how," she explained.

Rusty continued to drive occasionally, running a shopping service to and from Anchorage and Palmer with an army surplus Dodge car, then later hauling cargo in a newer Studebaker truck.

But now the "artist" in Rusty was coming out at full throttle. Painting was her third love, "after Russ and trucks." She had always dabbled a little here and there, but after visiting an art exhibit in Juneau after the war, her interest in painting was revived.

Rusty was a self-taught artist, experimenting with paints and reading art books for techniques. If she found something interesting in a book and wanted to learn more, she would just write to the author. She began corresponding with Stanley Woodward, a well-known Massachusetts artist, after asking for a fuller explanation of something in one of his books.

In the summer of 1949, Rusty flew to Boston for an art workshop with Mr. Woodward. The *Boston Sunday Post* gave a full page over to the story of the lady trucker and artist from Alaska. The reporter called her a "mighty Amazon," and described her driving feats with awe. Several photographs of Rusty with paints and easel accompanied the article, showing her in an uncharacteristically feminine blouse. In Alaska she usually wore a pair of men's slacks and a shirt because, as she explained, "Can't get the sleeves of most women's dresses over my muscles."

Armed with Mr. Woodward's advice and her expanding experience, Rusty returned to Alaska, where she continued to paint her favorite subjects of Alaskan landscapes and wildlife. She also developed a distinctive style using fluorescent paints that glowed under a black light. A beautiful example of this style showed a log cabin with Northern Lights that sparkled when the black light shone on them. One of her scenes of a bull moose in autumn was awarded Best of Valley Fair 1961, and she won prizes in other Alaska shows as well, such as the Fur Rendezvous in Anchorage.

Her painting repertoire also included portraits. She produced a fine rendition of "Abe Lincoln," as well as a noteworthy "Grandma Easi," an Eklutna native woman. And, of course, many portraits were of truckers with their trucks and construction engineers.

Both Rusty and Russ were active in community affairs in Palmer. They both belonged to the Elks Club. Rusty managed the art department at the Alaska State Fair in Palmer for fifteen years, and also taught art at the local college. Her artwork was popular with the community, and in 1983 she was honored with a showing of her paintings at the Alaska Historical and Transportation Museum in Palmer.

Rusty Dow brought to her adopted state the entrepreneurial attitude and adventurous spirit needed to survive and thrive there. With her trucking skills and her artistic talent, she fed both the economic and humanistic sides of the population, and she did it all with great humor.

Benzie Ola "Rusty" Dow died at the Valley Hospital in Palmer on June 18, 1989, at the age of ninety-five. Even though she spent the last several years of her life at the Palmer Pioneers' Home, driving a wheelchair instead of a truck, her indomitable spirit was always apparent. On the wall of her small room in the home was a bumper sticker that read, "I drove the Alaska Highway. Both ways, dammit."

ANFESIA SHAPSNIKOFF

1900–1973

Attu Weaver and Aleut Culture Keeper

ON JUNE 3, 1942, JAPANESE PLANES ATTACKED the U. S. military base at Dutch Harbor on Amaknak Island, on the north side of Unalaska. For two days bombs fell, and when it was over, thirty-five men had been killed. In the village near the base, there were no casualties among the local residents, who had taken refuge in air-raid shelters as instructed. This attack came almost exactly six months after the Japanese bombed Pearl Harbor.

On the sixth of June, Japanese forces invaded Attu, the most western island of the Aleutian Chain, a mere 750 miles from Japan. They captured forty-five Aleut natives and the government school-teacher, whose husband had died in the invasion. The prisoners were taken to an internment camp in Japan.

Shortly thereafter, the U.S. Navy evacuated the residents of Atka and burned their village to save it from Japanese occupation. Next, the Pribilof Islanders were evacuated, as were the residents of five smaller villages. The people of Unalaska knew that their turn would come and prepared as best they could.

Several men from the community packed belongings from the Church of the Holy Ascension. Father Dionecious removed items from the altar while Anfesia Shapsnikoff's son, Vincent Tutiakoff, kept a careful inventory of everything being crated. Because Anfesia was a reader for the church, she was responsible for packing the books and packed sixteen boxes.

The SS *Alaska* took the people from their homes. Each person could carry only one suitcase of belongings. Family heirlooms, photographs, and other items of irreplaceable value were hidden in their homes before the doors and windows were shut and locked. Reluctantly, Anfesia left behind the precious violin of her first husband, Michael Tutiakoff.

The ship deposited them in Wrangell, in southeast Alaska. From there they were moved to Burnett Inlet, a wilderness area between Wrangell and Ketchikan, where they found themselves surrounded by a forested world completely foreign from the wide-open landscapes of their homeland. There, they struggled to maintain their very existence in deplorable conditions. Many of the elderly died in that place, far from home. Although the Japanese troops were defeated the following year and there were no more hostilities in the Aleutians, it was three long years before the residents of Unalaska were returned to their island on April 22, 1945. Their homecoming was not a joyous one; they found their homes uninhabitable and ransacked, their valuables pilfered, and their church damaged.

"When we came [back] to Unalaska," Anfesia recalled, "we were happy and we were sad at the same time. Some of the homes were already deteriorating, windows broken, doors kicked in, personal belongings were gone. It made you feel like crying whenever someone got to go inside of their homes." The Aleut community had suffered severe blows, both physically and psychologically, from which it was unlikely they would completely recover.

Anchorage Museum of History and Art

ANFESIA SHAPSNIKOFF

Anfesia was born in Atka in 1900. When she was six years old, the family moved to Unalaska, then called Iliuliuk. Anfesia and her two brothers attended the Russian school there, where she learned to read Russian, as well as her own Aleut language. She also took classes at the government school, where she was taught English, along with such skills as cooking and sewing.

Anfesia was not a perfect student and told stories about having to kneel in front of an icon because she had not done her lessons. In later years she recalled that she had not been at all interested in learning to weave at school, as her mother, who was an expert Attu basket maker, wanted her to do. But her aunt was her teacher and would not let her say no, so she learned!

Anfesia's father died while she was a young teenager. When she was seventeen years old, Michael Tutiakoff, Anfesia's teacher in the Aleut language class, escorted her to choir practice in the winter, because her mother would not let her go out alone after dark. It was the next year, 1918, when Michael spoke to his father, telling him he would like to get married. He gave his father Anfesia's name, which his father gave to the Chief, Alexei Yatchmenoff, so that the marriage could be arranged. This was the native way, and the bride and groom usually did not know each other before the wedding.

As Anfesia slyly described it:

And so, when mother got word, she went and told my god-mother and I had one step ahead of them, because I had already talked this over with Mike Tutiakoff before this all happened. He got my okay before he went and asked his father to marry me. The Chief and the rest of the people didn't know about that. So, I went one step ahead of them. Anyways, it was a good marriage.

Soon after wedding plans had begun, Anfesia's mother, her aunt, and Michael's father were among forty-four residents who died during the devastating flu epidemic that swept through Unalaska between May 26 and June 13 of 1919. Therefore, the Chief finished the arrangements for the marriage and the wedding took place soon thereafter.

Anfesia and Mike raised one daughter, Martha; three sons, Vincent, Tracy, and Philemon; and an adopted son, Timothy. Another daughter, Mayme, died in infancy.

The first year of their marriage, Mike worked at a whaling station on Akutan, then cooked for sulfur miners on Akun. After that they returned to Unalaska, where he worked for the church and received a small salary. The family lived a subsistence lifestyle, in the native way. Anfesia referred to it as "going out and hustling for food." Ducks and seals were plentiful, and from a boat they could drop a line anywhere, anytime, and catch fish from the numerous codfish grounds in Unalaska Bay. They gathered sea urchins and clams along the beach. In the summer and fall, berries were plentiful in the hills, and gardens produced vegetables. The family worked hard. Anfesia said, "If we didn't put up our winter supply, why, then the children went hungry."

Mike was becoming more of a leader, both in the Aleut community and the Russian Orthodox Church. He had been the church secretary for many years and had helped the priest and teachers at the Russian school.

In 1932, he became a deacon and he might have gone on to become a priest. But in January of 1933, he traveled with the bishop aboard the ship, the *Umnak Native*. The vessel broke apart during a violent storm, and Michael Tutiakoff drowned.

The next few years were difficult for Anfesia and the children. The Unalaska Sisterhood and Brotherhood helped them with food; friends also shared provisions. Anfesia fished from the beach and sometimes caught enough salmon to exchange with Pribilof Islanders for seal meat. And, of course, she picked berries for jams and pies, and grew potatoes. Help came when Chief Alexei Yatchmenoff once more arranged a marriage for her. In February of 1937, Anfesia married Sergie Shapsnikoff, a widower.

Sergie not only provided for Anfesia and her children, but he and she adopted two more children, Kathryn and Gregory. The children called him "Friend."

About that time, the bishop of Alaska, Bishop Alexei, visited the Aleutians. When he came to Unalaska, he blessed Anfesia as a reader in the Church of the Holy Ascension, a position that elevated her standing in the community. As a reader, she was called on to communicate with the many outsiders and officials who began to swarm the island as construction began on Dutch Harbor, the military facility on Amaknak Island. She had also become an expert weaver of baskets in the Attu tradition, as her mother had been before her.

Then came the war and evacuation.

After their return home from southeast Alaska, Anfesia's community came together and began reassembling the pieces of their disheveled lives. Anfesia's second husband had drowned while fishing to provide food for the family, only one of the numerous casualties of the evacuation.

Although her son, Vincent Tutiakoff, was officially the Chairman and Recording Secretary of the Church Committee, it fell to Anfesia to write letters for the committee. With her command of English, she wrote about missing church papers and other items, and about church property and repairs. Father Dionecious had not come back to Unalaska, so she was called on to conduct church services and to assist visiting priests.

In 1947, Vincent drowned at the age of twenty-five. He was an officer in the Orthodox Brotherhood and had been in line to become a church leader. Anfesia became quite ill with tuberculosis of the spine, but recovered, despite dire predictions from her doctors.

The last two decades brought the burgeoning king crab industry and another influx of people and commercial building to Unalaska. Although the companies did hire local help and brought money into the community, the aftereffects continued to destroy the Aleut native way of life. When Anfesia was a little girl growing up in Unalaska, she could drink clean water right from the creek, pick berries from the hills, and gather clams, mussels, and sea urchins on the beach. Because of pollution from the canneries and the ruins from the war, these simple pastimes were no longer easily accomplished.

Anfesia also recognized that the young people weren't interested in pursuing the subsistence lifestyle, even if it were still possible. Many of them had turned their eyes Outside. They wanted jobs and the things that money could buy. She intensified her efforts to pass on the Aleut language and her skill of basket weaving to the next generation. By working with visiting linguists and anthropologists, she hoped to assure an accurate preservation of her people's language and traditions.

Anfesia's grandson, Vincent—known to his family as Buddy—eventually moved in with her. In 1956 she again became ill, and had to go to the hospital in Anchorage. Buddy stayed at the Baptist Mission in Kodiak until she was able to return three months later.

Anfesia had been communicating with the historical society in Kodiak, and after she recovered from her illness, she traveled there and gave the first of many basket-weaving classes. Her first class in 1957 consisted of nine students, and she returned to give classes there off and on for several years.

One summer she was giving a class in Kodiak during the historical society's outdoor theatre production of the *Cry of the Wild Ram*. The historical drama celebrated Alaska's Russian heritage, particularly the Russian colony on Kodiak. Anfesia was recruited to perform in the play.

"I'm the Aleut they found," she said, laughing.

She was supposed to squat down and weave a basket. Of course, to be authentic to the time, she couldn't wear her glasses, so decided to weave a fish basket because the weave was larger. As she still couldn't see well enough to weave, her class members would work on it some each day until they finished it for her.

"It was in display in Anchorage and it looked real nice and it was bought afterwards," she reported when telling the story.

In 1959, Alaska Governor William A. Egan put Anfesia in charge of the Alaska Booth at the Oregon Centennial in Portland. She took her "demonstration" basket, which she used in her classes, and was delighted when Senator John F. Kennedy held it in his hands and spoke with her. During the next few years, she traveled and gave talks and demonstrations in California and Arizona.

In the summer of 1967, Anfesia was invited to speak to the Resurrection Bay Historical Society in Seward as part of their

Alaska Centennial Celebration. She told the group it was the first time she had given her presentation in Alaska. From Seward she traveled to Anchorage and Juneau, speaking, giving basket-weaving demonstrations, and, in Anchorage, even appearing on television.

From Anchorage she wrote to Margaret Hafemeister in Seward, "Busy, busy. I didn't know it would turn out this way, but I am wanted here and there. . . . Seems as if everyone knows me here, even the priest."

As part of the statewide Alaska Centennial Celebration in 1967, Anfesia was given the Governor's Award for perpetuating native arts and crafts through her basketry.

But even as the state was praising her, it was creating another tragedy in her community. That summer a social worker came to Unalaska bearing a list of about twenty children who were to be removed from their homes and raised in more "civilized" conditions. This was an affront to the Aleuts, and Anfesia took it personally.

She protested the policy and wrote to her friend, Ray Hudson, "I have written Juneau and told them what is happening. . . . I let them know Unalaska could keep neglected children too like elsewhere so they could know of their native ways, so Aleuts could be restored. . . ."

The welfare of Aleut children had always been one of Anfesia's primary concerns. She served several terms on the Unalaska City Council and was on the city's first Board of Health. In that capacity she contributed to the organization of the Iliuliuk Family and Health Services, incorporated in 1971 and still the primary health agency for the community.

Anfesia deeply lamented the declining interest of her people in speaking Aleut and maintaining their traditions. Hoping to preserve as much as possible, Anfesia went to the University of Alaska in Fairbanks, where she taught Aleut dancing as well as basket-weaving, and recorded songs and stories. In fact, one of her last trips was to

Fairbanks to work with the Alaska Native Languages Program, developing the Atka and Unalaska dialects.

Back in Unalaska, she gave basket-weaving classes from her home. She spoke to students about her childhood and native customs, and she sang to them and told them traditional stories. A booklet encompassing her childhood Christmas memories was distributed to Unalaska school children at Russian Christmas in January of 1972.

For several weeks, beginning in November of 1969, she inserted in *The Unalaskan* newspaper an item in Aleut. Underneath the first one it said in English, "If you don't understand this, learn it! And ask what it means." For the second and successive weeks, she included the translation for the previous week.

The item for the week of November 17 read:

Iig^akun tutalix aqaning waya malgakun ang^achin aqatalgaqan-gin–Ulux^waya galix tanax ama angachisin sulakyn. Malix miimiin tununalgilix. Tunuxtan.

Anfesia wrote Aleut in The Cyrillic script developed in the 1820s. This rendition is written in Roman letters. Each little cap goes above the letter preceding it. Here is the translation for the item:

Things I heard of long ago are happening. Unknown people are coming, taking over our land and the things we made our living with. So let's get together and prevent these, by speaking up.

Those long-ago predictions were certainly beginning to come true in 1970. The U.S. government planned to sell the land that it had claimed to build military facilities on Amaknak Island and surrounding the village. Anfesia blamed the military for much of the pollution of traditional fishing grounds. She would not stand by and let them take away the land, too. She had served on the Board of Equalization, and feared that the Aleuts would be forced to pay taxes on the land where they lived.

In January of 1971, the government sale was stopped by a civil lawsuit on behalf of Anfesia Shapsnikoff, Nick Peterson, and Henry Swanson, the eldest residents of Unalaska. In December President Richard Nixon signed the Alaska Native Claims Act. The land for sale on Amaknak and Unalaska Islands now belonged to the Aleut people.

In December of 1972, although ill and growing weaker, Anfesia supervised the cleaning of the interior of the Cathedral of the Holy Ascension in preparation for Christmas services. She had done this many times before as a member and officer of the Sister-hood. She recognized the importance of this church, both as a place of worship and as a building of great historic significance. The cathedral is on the National Register of Historic Places and is a National Historic Landmark.

The following January, Anfesia baptized her great-grandson, Vincent Michael Jr., although she was too weak to lift the baby the customary three times and had to perform the baptism in her home. She continued to weaken and died on the airplane taking her to the Native Hospital in Anchorage on January 15. She is buried in the church graveyard beside Alexei Yatchmenoff.

Anfesia's influence in the Aleut community endures after her death. Children she instructed in the teachings of her church have become important members of the congregation. Her passion for Aleut culture has infused various Aleut organizations, and her will-ingness to serve on civic boards has inspired others to follow her example. The basket-weaving classes continued to flourish in Kodiak, and in 2005 Hazel Jones, who was one of Anfesia's students in the early 1970s, taught the class. Anfesia received many awards and honors, including honorary lifetime memberships in the Res-urrection Bay Historical Society and Kodiak Historical Society, and a special certificate from Bishop Theodosius for her long and out-standing service to the Orthodox faith.

Three weeks after her death, "Senate Concurrent Resolution No. 24 in the Legislature of the State of Alaska, Eighth Legislature—First Session: Honoring Anfesia Shapsnikoff" was read into the record on February 6, 1973. It concluded:

> BE IT RESOLVED by the Alaska Legislature that it expresses its most profound sense of loss as a result of the death of this truly remarkable "Little Grandma" but affirms its belief that, because of her devotion to her people, her culture, her community, and her state, generations of Alaskans for years to come will be indebted to Anfesia Shapsnikoff and she will always be revered as a truly great Alaskan.

BIBLIOGRAPHY

General References

Davis, Mary Lee. *Uncle Sam's Attic.* Boston: W. A. Wilde Co., 1930.

———. *We Are Alaskans.* Boston: W. A. Wilde Co., 1931.

Gruening, Ernest. *The State of Alaska.* New York: Random House, 1954.

Murphy, Claire Rudolf and Jane G. Haigh. *Gold Rush Women.* Portland: Alaska Northwest Books, 2001.

———. *Gold Rush Dogs.* Portland: Alaska Northwest Books, 1997.

Romig, Emily Craig. *The Life and Travels of a Pioneer Woman in Alaska.* Caldwell, Idaho: Caxton Printers, 1945.

Tanana-Yukon Historical Society. *First Catch Your Moose: The Fairbanks Cookbook, 1909: A Facsimile Reprint of the 1909 Edition of Fairbanks Cook Book of Tested Recipes.* Fairbanks, Alaska: Tanana-Yukon Historical Society, 1999.

Willoughby, Barrett. *Alaskans All.* Freeport, N.Y.: Books for Libraries Press, 1971.

Harriet Smith Pullen

Allen, Lois H. *Skagway Cheechako.* February 20, 1937.

———. "He Takes 'Em For a Ride." *Alaska Sportsman.* September 1940.

Branham, Bud. "Gold-Rush Mother." *Alaska Sportsman.* August 1940.

Davis, Mary Lee. *Uncle Sam's Attic.* Boston: W. A. Wilde Co., 1930.

Limmer, Eleanor. "Harriet Pullen, Skagway Entrepreneur." *Alaska Sportsman*. August 1977.

Munsey, Sylvia Falconer. "Ma Pullen, Mother of the North." *Great Lander Shopping News*. September 29, 1971.

Murphy, Claire Rudolf and Jane G. Haigh. *Gold Rush Women*. Portland: Alaska Northwest Books, 1997.

Selmer, Maxine. Correspondence with author, February 2005.

Willoughby, Barrett. *Alaskans All*. Freeport, N.Y.: Books for Libraries Press, 1971.

Matilda Kinnon "Tillie" Paul Tamaree

Davis, Mary Lee. *We Are Alaskans*. Boston: W. A. Wilde Co., 1931.

DeGermain, Frances Paul. Correspondence with author, September–October 2004.

DeWitt, Marion Paul. Interview with author, September 7, 2004.

Estus, Nana Paul. Correspondence with author, October 5, 2004.

Paul, Frances Lackey. *Kahtahah*. Anchorage, Alaska: Northwest Publishing Co., 1976.

Ricketts, Nancy J. "Matilda Kinnon Paul Tamaree/Kahtahah: Kahtliyudt." *Haa Kusteeyi; Our Culture: Tlingit Life Stories*. Edited by Nora Marks Dauenhauer and Richard Dauenhauer. Seattle: University of Washington Press, 1994.

Sherr, Lynn and Jurate Kazickas. *Susan B. Anthony Slept Here*. New York: Random House, 1994.

Verdesi, Elizabeth Howell and Sylvia Thorson-Smith. *A Sampler of Saints; In praise of our Presbyterian foremothers, no longer forgotten, written to commemorate the Bicentennial of the Presbyterian Church (U.S.A.)*. Presbyterian Historical Society, 1988.

The Verstovian. "Mrs. William Tamaree Dies at Wrangell." September, 1952.

The Wrangell Sentinel. "Mrs. William Tamaree, Wrangell Pioneer, Taken by Death." August 22, 1952.

Bundtzen, Thomas K. "A History of Mining in the Kantishna Hills." *Alaska Journal.* Volume 8, Spring 1978.

Burford, Virgil. *North to Danger.* Caldwell, Idaho: Caxton, 1969.

Carson, Ruth. "Joe and Fannie Quigley." *Alaska Sportsman.* April 1970.

Davis, Mary Lee. *We Are Alaskans.* Boston: W. A. Wilde Co., 1931.

Fannie Quigley Collection. Archives, Alaska and Polar Regions Department, Elmer E. Rasmuson Library, University of Alaska, Fairbanks.

Haigh, Jane G. "Searching for Fannie Quigley." *Fairbanks Daily News-Miner.* Five-part series. May 9, 1999; May 23, 1999; May 30, 1999; June 6, 1999; June 30, 1999.

Murphy, Claire Rudolf and Jane G. Haigh. *Gold Rush Women.* Portland: Alaska Northwest Books, 1997.

Pearson, Grant H. *My Life of High Adventure.* New York: Prentice-Hall, 1962.

———. "Fannie Quigley, Frontierswoman." *Alaska Sportsman.* August 1947.

Sheldon, Charles. *The Wilderness of Denali.* New York: Charles Scribner's Sons, 1930.

University of Alaska, Fairbanks, Web site. "Ruth Barrack-Long Time UA Supporter," http://www.alaska.edu/opa/eInfo/index.xml?StoryID=302.

U.S. Department of the Interior Web site. "The History of Kantishna: Kantishna Pioneers," http://www.nps.gov/dena/home/historyandculture/kanhx/kantishna_pioneers.htm.

Zanjani, Sally Springmeyer. *A Mine of Her Own: Women Prospectors in the American West, 1850–1950.* Lincoln: University of Nebraska Press, 1997.

Margaret Keenan Harrais

Gruening, Ernest. *The State of Alaska*. New York: Random House, 1954.

Margaret Harrais Collection. Box 1, Folders 1, 2, 4, 6, 10. Archives, Alaska and Polar Regions Department, Rasmuson Library, University of Alaska, Fairbanks.

Munsey, Sylvia Falconer. "Margaret Keenan Harrais." *Alaska Journal*. Summer 1975.

Tewkesbury's Who's Who in Alaska and Alaska Business Index. Juneau: Tewkesbury Publishers, 1947.

Nellie Neal Lawing

Allen, Lois Hudson. "Woman Unafraid." *Alaska Sportsman*. July 1939.

Anchorage Times. "Famed Alaska Nellie is Dead at Age of 84." May 11, 1956.

Capra, Douglas. *Into Alaska A Woman Came: A Play Based on the Life of Alaska Nellie*. Unpublished manuscript, 2003. First produced in Seward, Alaska, March 2003.

————. Correspondence with author, January, February 2005.

————. Interview with author, December 2004.

————. "Legend of Alaska Nellie as Big as the State Itself." Seward, Alaska: Seward Visitor Guide, 1996.

Jones, Grace C. "Christmas at Alaska Nellie's." *Alaska Sportsman*. December 1963.

Lawing, Nellie Neal. *Alaska Nellie*. Seattle: Chieftain Press. Seattle Printing and Publishing Co., 1940.

Olthius, Diane. *Lawing: Alaska Nellie's Stabilization Plan*. Kenai Mountains–Turnagain Arm Corridor Communications Association: Alaska Nellie's Historical Society, 2003.

————. Interview with author, September 7, 2004.

Pierce, Carrie Ida. "I Remember Nellie." *Alaska Sportsman*. January 1957.

Rhodes, Herb. "Alaska Nellie: A Florence Nightingale of the North." *The Great Lander Shopping News*. August 27, 1975.

Lois Hudson Allen

Allen, Barbara. Correspondence with author, October, December, 2004.

Allen, Jamie. "My great grandmother Lois Hudson Allen." 2005 on-line genealogy, http://freepages.genealogy.rootsweb.com/~jamesdow/ameret.htm.

Allen, Lois Hudson. "Woman Unafraid." *Alaska Sportsman*. July 1939.

———. "Sourdough Governor." *Alaska Sportsman*. December 1939.

———. "He Takes 'Em For a Ride." *Alaska Sportsman*. September 1940.

———. "Matanuska Gets Down to Business." *Alaska Sportsman*. October 1941.

Moose Pass Miner. March 28, 1939–February 24, 1940.

Olthius, Diane. "Peninsula author helps shape area history: Forging frontiers." *Kenai Peninsula Clarion*. February 10, 2002.

——— and others (eds.). *Alaska's Kenai Peninsula: The Road We've Traveled*. Hope, Alaska: Kenai Peninsula Historical Society, 2002.

———. Interview with author, September 7, 2004.

The Skagway Cheechako. November 21, 1936–May 27, 1938.

Josephine Sather

Capra, Doug. "The Story of Mrs. Herring Pete of Nuka Island." Seward, Alaska: Seward Visitor's Guide, 1998.

———. Correspondence with author, July 2005.

Dehlin, Mary Ann. "Mrs. Sather Leaves Nuka." *Anchorage Daily Times*. June 12, 1962.

Norris, Frank and Linda Cook. *A Stern and Rock-Bound Coast: Kenai Fjords National Park Historic Resource Study.* National Park Service, 2002.

Norris, Frank B. "Monarchs of the Kenai Coast." *Alaska.* May/June 2001.

Petticoat Gazette. "Death takes Mrs. 'Herring Pete' and so ends the saga of Nuka Island." Seward, Alaska. October 22, 1964.

Sather, Josephine. "The Island; The first of four chapters of 'Fox Farm at Nuka Bay'." *Alaska Sportsman.* July 1946.

———. "The Foxes; The second of four chapters of 'Fox Farm at Nuka Bay'." *Alaska Sportsman.* August 1946.

———. "The Birds and the Bears; the third of four chapters of 'Fox Farm at Nuka Bay'." *Alaska Sportsman.* September 1946.

———. "Our Glorious World; The last of four chapters of 'Fox Farm at Nuka Bay'." Alaska Sportsman. October 1946.

———. Untitled and unpublished autobiography manuscript. Collection of Doug Capra, Seward, Alaska.

Crystal Brilliant Snow Jenne

Chandonnet, Ann. "A Persistent Pioneer." *The Juneau Empire.* January 14, 2004.

Murphy, Claire Rudolf and Jane G. Haigh. *Gold Rush Women.* Portland: Alaska Northwest Books, 1997.

Schneider, Rose. *The Snow Family of Juneau, Alaska: A Guide to the Papers and Photographs.* Juneau, Alaska: Alaska Department of Education, 1992.

Snow Family Collection. Archives, Alaska State Museum, Juneau.

Jessie Spiro Bloom

Farthest North Girl Scout Council website. "Jessie Bloom." http://home.gci.net/~fngsc/Jessie_Bloom.htm.

Girl Scouts in Alaska: Spanning Six Decades. 1925–1985. Fairbanks: Farthest North Girl Scout Council, 1985.

Movius, Phyllis Demuth. *The Role of Women in the Founding and Development of Fairbanks, Alaska, 1903–1923*. Ann Arbor, Mich.: University Microfilms International, 1997.

Robert and Jessie Bloom Papers. Box 5, Folders 30, 31, 32, 33. Box 7, Folder 90. Archives, Alaska and Polar Regions Department, Rasmuson Library, University of Alaska, Fairbanks.

Clara Hickman Rust

Clara Rust Collection. Box 1, Folder 22. Box 6, Folder 192. Box 7, Folder 233. Archives, Alaska and Polar Regions Department, Rasmuson Library, University of Alaska, Fairbanks.

Rust, Clara H. "The 'Hello Girls' of Bygone Days." *Alaska Sportsman*. January 1964.

———. "I Was a Bride on the Little Eldorado; Part One." *Alaska Sportsman*. March 1963.

———. "I Was a Bride on the Little Eldorado; Part Two." *Alaska Sportsman*. April 1963.

———. "To Fairbanks by Steamboat." *Alaska Journal*. Winter 1971.

Wilson, Ingeborg B. "Clara Hickman Rust: Greenest Bride on the Creeks." *Great Lander Shopping News*. October 25, 1972.

Wold, Jo Anne. *This Old House: The Story of Clara Rust, Alaska Pioneer*. Anchorage: Alaska Northwest Publishing Company, 1976.

Benzie Ola "Rusty" Dow

The Anchorage Times. "Legendary 'redheaded ball of energy,' Rusty Dow, dies." June 20, 1989.

Brooks, Maria. Transcript, Oral history interview with Rusty Dow at Pioneer Home, Palmer, Alaska, August 3, 1980. Rusty Dow Collection. Archives and Manuscript Department, Consortium Library, University of Alaska, Anchorage.

Dow, Marilyn DeVine. Correspondence with author, November, December 2004.

Dow, Rusty. Handwritten manuscript detailing drive from Fairbanks to Dawson Creek. Undated, unpublished. Circa June 1944. Rusty Dow Collection. Archives and Manuscript Department, Consortium Library, University of Alaska. Anchorage.

The Forty-ninth Star. "Alaska's Lady Trucker Takes Boston in Tow." August 14, 1949.

Frey, Lucille. "Trucker with a Palette." *Anchorage Daily News.* June 9, 1983.

Hood, Lela Latch. "The Lady Drives a Truck." *Great Lander Shopping News.* October 15, 1975.

Schmitt, Nancy Cain. "Pioneer Truck Driver Finds Life Boring." *The Anchorage Times.* September 2, 1979.

Anfesia Shapsnikoff

Anfesia Shapsnikoff Collection. Box 1, Folders 15, 17, 18. Archives, Alaska and Polar Regions Department, Rasmuson Library, University of Alaska, Fairbanks.

Baranov Museum Web site. "Attu Grass Basket Weaving with Hazel Jones." http://www.baranov.us/events.html.

Hudson, Ray. *Moments Rightly Placed: An Aleutian Memoir.* Kenmore, Washington: Epicenter Press, 1998.

————. Correspondence with author, July 25, 2005.

Letters from Anfesia Shapsnikoff, 1967. Margaret Hafemeister Collection, Archives and Manuscript Department, Consortium Library, University of Alaska, Anchorage.

Neseth, Eunice. Transcript, Oral History Interview at interviewer's home, Kodiak, Alaska, May 21, 1971. Anfesia Shapsnikoff Collection, Archives and Manuscript Department, Consortium Library, University of Alaska, Anchorage.

Oleksa, Rev. Michael. *Six Alaskan Native Women Leaders: Pre-Statehood.* Alaska State Department of Education, January 1991.

Unugulux Tunusangin, Oldtime Stories. Unalaska City School District, Unalaska, Alaska.

ABOUT THE AUTHOR

Cherry Lyon Jones, a Colorado College alumnus, has been a pre-school/parent education teacher, has owned and operated a children's bookstore, is a storyteller, and does portrayals of historical women. A native Texan, she has spent her adult life in California, Nevada and, now, Alaska in the summers. History has always been her avocation, and reading, her great pleasure. She belongs to the Society of Children's Book Writers and Illustrators and the Nevada Women's History Project.